Stitches in Time

Doll Costumes and Accessories, 1850-1925

Florence Theriault

Gold Horse Publishing

To order additional copies:
Dollmasters, PO Box 2319, Annapolis, MD 21404
Telephone: (800) 966-3655 Fax (410) 224-2515

Research by Linda Phipps
Special thank you to Natalie Stewart
Art Direction and Design by David Hirner
Photography by Robert Bartlett

$39
ISBN: 0-912823-59-3
Printed in Hong Kong

Table of Contents

Introduction

The wealthy grand dame visited the famous French milliner. "I simply must have a new chapeaux for an afternoon affair", she proclaimed, "and I must have it today." The milliner said this was impossible, but after threats and cajoling by the grand dame, finally agreed to the rush deadline.

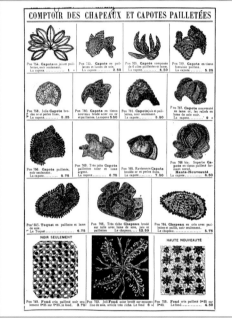

The straw bonnets were destined to be covered with silk, lace, feathers and flowers, but even then variations in basic shape and form were important.

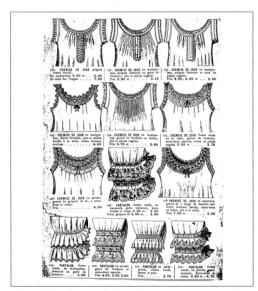

As machine lace and trims became more generally available, even lingerie was offered in fabulous variations on a same basic theme, this 1894 catalogue illustration shows.

Later that day the grand dame returned to the milliner's. She was delighted with her new bonnet. And then the milliner told her the price.

"That is impossible!", she cried, "How could just this ribbon and straw be such a great price?" The milliner simply looked at her, saying nothing. Then he removed the bonnet from her head, deftly unwound the ribbons, handed them to her in a pile and murmured "Madame, the ribbon is free."

While, strictly speaking, the "ribbon" of 19th-century costumes was far from free, the story does vividly illustrate that the workmanship of the couturiers and milliners was their tour de force. Through the skillful and deft manipulation of fabrics couturiers were able to construct costumes that were virtual works of art; techniques such as ruching, cording, cartridge pleating and vandyking concerned the basic fabric itself rather than the superimposition of alien trim. Even concerning bonnets, variations in the basic form could achieve totally different looks.

Partly, this was a result of the use of very fine fabrics (the ribbon, actually, was not free!), those that could be draped, folded, quilted, padded or pleated in a myriad of ways to form elegant shapes. But mostly, it was a result of construction - that best of construction which appears utterly simple and effortless, yet is quite complicated.

This is not to say that the imposition of alien fabrics, trims, lace and embroidery did not enhance the costumes. Indeed, as the century wore along, couturiers made more and more use of the luxe decorations that were available to them. The development of machine-made lace allowed its lavish use, as did the "new" silks in vivid colors coming from the French silk mills in Lyon and elsewhere.

Fashions for adult women were re-created in diminutive form for children; during certain epochs the styles were modified to accommodate childish activities while at other times they were virtual mirrors of "big people" clothes.

That is also true of doll costumes. These miniature models of people-fashion have, increasingly, become collected by fashion historians who despair at storing and preserving full-size antique costumes. While it is true that compromises were sometimes made in the production of "plaything" clothing, it is also true that the small costumes echo the fabrics, the styles and the decoration of actual people-fashions. Even the couturiers of the era bear out that fact; from Worth, the renowned 19th-century couturier who also created doll clothing, to the famous Paris department stores of the end of the century who advertised "Articles pour Poupees" smack in the middle of a page of childrens' clothing.

As collecting of doll costumes becomes more seriously approached, and as prices of these rare little objects increase, knowledge concerning age and authenticity becomes more and more important. Thus this book has arranged costumes in a chronological manner so that stylistic and decorative changes can be more readily observed. Each of the costumes presented in this book was actually constructed in the given period in which it is presented that is, the costume is not simply a contemporary re-creation of an old costume from period fabrics.

While it is certain that collectors will wish to use these costumes in the presentation of their dolls, it is also hoped, by the author, that rare and fine examples will be preserved in a fabric-friendly environment. So few of these beautiful works still remain!

Production of doll costumes became an entire industry unto itself, as shown in this 1910 holiday catalog from the Parisian Louvre department store.

"Articles for poupees" were offered right alongside children's clothing, and, in fact, were virtual miniature versions of the "real people" clothing, in a 1910 Paris catalogue.

An accurate study of historic fashion can be accomplished by the collection and study of antique doll costumes. As this 1872 engraving from Magasin des Demoiselles illustrates, children's clothing was often simply a miniaturization of adult clothing, and doll clothing was yet a further miniaturization of child clothing. Not only were the material, form and fashion nearly identical, but so were the construction techniques, both visible and hidden.

CHAPTER ONE

Early Costumes.
The Restoration or
Empire Era,
1830-1855.

**1. IVORY TULLE GOWN
WITH LACE BODICE**
3 1/2" shoulder width. 6" waist.
13" skirt length. Hand-made ivory
lace bodice with dainty floral
pattern and scalloped edge, English
net short sleeves, full-length
English net full skirt-over-ivory
silk underdress. Tarlatan
underlining, red silk sash. The
costume is sewn together,
originally, onto muslin body on
which it appears. To accommodate
the short-sleeved gown the paper
mache arms have painted above-
the-elbow fingerless gloves.

**2. JACONET COTTON BABY
GOWN**
5 1/2" shoulder width. 11" waist.
25" skirt length. Baby gown, of
fine sheet jaconet cotton has
rounded low neckline, pouf short
sleeves with elaborate dart and V-
insert at under arms, full bodice,
extended skirt with tiny cartridge
pleats at waist, six hook and eye
closures. There is lace trim on the
sleeves and cording at the neckline,
shoulders and waist. Entirely
hand-stitched with tiniest of
stitches.

3. WHITE BATISTE DRESS WITH SHIRRED BODICE
4" shoulders. 7 1/2" waist. 10" skirt length. The simple dress has fitted bodice with ten horizontal bands of shirring in graduated widths at both front and back of dress, corded and bound neckline, fitted waist with V-shaped band, very full skirt with cartridge pleats, long sleeves, six hook and eye closures. A 2" underpanel below the waist reinforces the skirt fullness created by the cartridge pleats.

4. COTTON ORGANDY PATTERNED GOWN
4 1/2" shoulder width. 9" waist. 13" skirt length. Designed to be worn over blouse, the rose cotton organdy day gown has surplice-type bodice with full dart shaping and lace trim, split short sleeves which are set-in and corded, outlined with lace. The waist is fitted and closes at the left side with hook and eye. The skirt is fuller in back from a multitude of tiny cartridge pleats.

5. RED KID SLIPPERS
1 3/4". Red soft kidskin slippers have red silk binding, red silk ribbon trim, tan undersoles.

6. RED VELVET BAG
2 1/4". Six-sided rectangular bag with slight padding has metallic gold braid outline and handle, decorative medallion center with applique beads and braid.

Early Costumes. The Restoration or Empire Era, 1830-1855.

7. WHITE COTTON DOTTED DRESS

3 1/2" shoulder width. 6 1/4" waist. 6 1/2" L. Crisp white cotton dress with robin's egg blue dotted pattern has squared neckline with tucks at shoulders, full bodice, banded fitted waistline, pouffed sleeves with corded banding, full skirt with tiny tight gathers at waistline, very full skirt with hem ruffle, two pearl buttons, hook and eye closure at waist.

8. TWO EARLY DRESSES WITH PANTALOONS

Each 3" shoulder width, 5 3/4" waist, 6-7" length. Comprising brown plaid cotton percale frock with self-piping at waist and peasant sleeves, very tiny full gathers at waist; and multi-patterned frock with printed muslin top and striped calico skirt, bishop sleeves, tiny cuffs, cartridge pleated skirt, lined waist band; and two pairs of early trimmed pantaloons.

9. THREE COTTON PETTICOATS

Each about 7" waist. 7" length. Comprising stiffened cambric with blue abstract pattern and lined hem, pleated waist; cotton gingham plaid with set-in waist in front, draw-string gathers at back, gathered dust ruffle of same fabric; and white muslin with gathered wasit, set-in waist band, Valenciennes lace trim at hemline. Customarily multiple petticoats were worn, for various purposes of style, warmth and/or modesty.

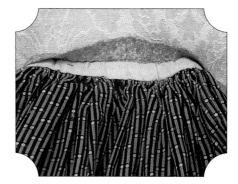

Early Costumes. The Restoration or Empire Era, 1830-1855.

10. PURPLE CALICO PRINT DRESS AND PANTALOONS

4" shoulder width. 7" waist. 10 1/2" skirt length. Calico dress with very tiny purple leaf pattern has rounded neck with drawstring cording, dropped shoulders with cording at shoulder seams and cuffs, set-in long sleeves with tiny pearl button closures, unusual cording down center bodice and V-shaped waistline, all-around cartridge pleated skirt with very full skirt, six hook and eye closures. And muslin pantaloons, 7" waist, 10 1/2" length, with rich Swiss embroidered lace and ruffles.

10A. MUSLIN DAY GOWN WITH HIDDEN FITTED BODICE

4" shoulder width. 14" overall length. White muslin gown with simple floral print is loosely fitted in front, hiding an attached dart-fitted muslin chemise with eight hook and eye closures, balloon upper sleeve with cartridge pleats at shoulders, fitted lower sleeves with 1" lace cuffs, V-shaped large collar with 1" lace and stand-up neck collar. The back is dart-fitted with reverse box pleat extending into long train, dust ruffle on skirt, double rows of silk ribbon.

11. WIRED MUSLIN BONNET AND CHAMBRAY APRON

5" x 6" exterior size. 2" interior head width. An outwardly simple bonnet is elaborately wired: three graduated size rings supporting three vertical bands. The armature is covered with delicate floral muslin pattern in pleated and tiered matter, box-pleated and pinked edging, long-self ties and streamers. And purple/blue chambray apron with cartridge pleats, two square pockets.

12. GREEN NEEDLEPOINT SLIPPERS

2 1/2". Pale green needlepoint slippers with muslin lining have hand-stitched dark green ribbon binding, hand-stitched soles, purple velvet ribbon trim with tiny silver buckles. The day slippers were offered in doll boutiques of 1860 Paris.

13. BROWN CALICO GOWN, APRON AND CALASH BONNET
4" shoulder width. 7" waist. 9 3/4" skirt length. Brown patterned calico cotton gown has fitted
bodice with corded detail at neckline, center seam, dropped shoulders of set-in sleeves and V-shaped waist. The skirt has tiny cartridge pleats and
is very full. There are seven hook and eye closures, draw-string at neckline, buttoned cuffs. A patterned apron with tie-strings and calash bonnet of
cotton muslin, collapsible, with vandyked detail of bavolet (bonnet is stained but essential rare shape and intricate construction is retained).

14. WOVEN MARKET BASKET
5" H. including handles. The loosely-woven market basket is of cord with intricate openwork on body, tight weave on base, braided handles.

15. PARCHMENT-COVERED DOMED TRAVELING TRUNK
4" L. A firm-sided trunk with domed top is covered with parchment-like paper to emulate leather,
has red leather horizontal bands with metal studs, bail handles at sides, metal faux-clasp. When
opened, the interior (quite worn) has red and green paper lining, three compartments, two
lids.

16. TAN LEATHER SHOES
3 1/4". Firm-soled tan leather shoes have sturdy seaming, thick leather soles
and heels, loafer-like flap over top of foot, leather bow with silver buckle
trim. The commercially-made shoes are of finest quality and may have
been produced as salesman's samples.

17. COTTON MUSLIN GOWN WITH CAP AND CHEMISE
7" shoulders. 13" waist. 14 3/4" skirt length. Cotton muslin gown with delicate woven leaf and star-scroll pattern in browns and reds has rounded neckline, with dropped shoulders, cartridge pleated sleeves with fullness at shoulders and tapering to cuffed wrists with hook and eye closures, full bodice, set in 1" waist band with cording at top edge, flatter skirt in front, very full skirt from cartridge pleats at back. The muslin-lined bodice has draw-string closure at neck, two brass hook and eye closures at waist; a 5" muslin lining at hemline gives shape to skirt fullness. And muslin under-cap with pale purple print, seam-shaping, ties at front and back, fully lined. And matching full slip of heavy muslin with Maltese lace, dart-fitted bodice, cartridge pleated skirt.

18. MIDNIGHT PURPLE SILK PINAFORE AND BROCADE CAP
7" shoulders. 8" waist. 11" skirt length. Very fine, yet crisp, Habutai silk pinafore of dense midnight purple with slight iridescence, has surplice bodice with cording, set-in waist with double hook and eye closure, wing-like gathered bretelles, vandyke detail on bretelles, along hem, and down the entire open back, two rounded pockets with vertical pleating and corded edges. And aubergine pongee silk cap with ruched trim in black georgette, purple cord ties, silk lining.

19. WHITE DIMITY GOWN WITH BONNET AND PANTALOONS

6" shoulders. 11" waist. 14" skirt length. White dimity gown with woven vertical bands has high waist, 1 1/2" waist band, very full surplice bodice from cartridge pleats at shoulders, set-in shoulder bands of corded edge gathering (see photo detail), exaggerated gigot sleeves with corded edging, fitted cuffs, very full cartridge pleated skirt, 3 1/2" hem. And matching pantaloons with 11" waist and 17" length, are of batiste to knees, dimity below the knees with pleated lace edged trim at ankles. And dimity bonnet with fitted medallion back, V-shaping at ears with extended ties, nainsook ruffle with finished scalloped edging, adjustable-size ties at back.

20. BLUE SILK TWILL SLIPPERS

4" L. Hand-sewn blue silk twill soft shoes or slippers are muslin lined, have paler blue silk binding, blue ribbon ties, soft tan leather one-piece soles with four tiny tacks.

21. DOTTED SWISS BONNET WITH EMBROIDERY

Adjustable size to fit about 4" head width. Draw-string bonnet of dotted Swiss with inset medallion of embroidered English net, ruffled English net crown. Designed to fit head with drawstrings.

Early Costumes. The Restoration or Empire Era, 1830-1855.

22. RED CALICO GOWN WITH GIGOT SLEEVES
8" shoulder width, 13 3/4" waist, 13" skirt length. Of patterned red cotton calico with abstract pattern, the gown has narrow yoke with corded detail, full gathers below held by self-fabric belt, cording at neckline, very full gigot sleeves corded at seamline and cuffs, muslin lining at neckline, back yoke and sleeves, overcast finished interior seams.

23. BLEACHED MUSLIN PINAFORE
8" shoulder width, 14" waist, 11 3/4" skirt length. Fine bleached muslin pinafore has cartridge pleated full skirt, set-in waist, wide bretelles, two pockets, vandyking trim along the bottom edge of bretelles, pockets, hemline, back sides; hook and eye closure, fine hand-sewing details.

24. MUSLIN PETTICOAT AND CHEMISETTE
8" shoulder width, 11 1/4" waist, 14" skirt length. Heavy muslin petticoat has box pleats at front, cartridge pleating at back, set-in waist band, hook and eye closure; with sheer muslin chemisette with wide Dutch collar, pearl button closure; each in fine hand sewing.

CHAPTER TWO.
Mid-Century Costumes, 1855-1875

25. WHITE NAINSOOK GOWN AND UNDERGARMENTS
5 1/2" shoulder width. 12" waist. 12 1/2" skirt length. Comprises gown of white nainsook with muslin-lined fitted bodice having shirred plastron of self-fabric edged with lace, V-shaped waist with piping, lace-trimmed piped neckline, trumpet sleeves with double tier of lace, very full skirt with seven horizontal tucks. With dotted swiss sacque with rounded collar, bell sleeves, side godets for back fullness, lace edging. And 10" length slim pantaloons with double tucks and drawstring waist; 12 1/2" L. bleached muslin petticoat with fitted cartridge-pleated waist; 16" L. bleached muslin chemise with drawstring neckline and tatted sleeves.

Mid-Century Costumes, 1855-1875.

15

26. SILK BENGALINE GOWN AND VEST
3 1/2" shoulder width. 9" waist. 8 1/2" skirt length. One-piece gown with fitted muslin-lined bodice, Princess-style darts at back bodice, royal blue piping at neckline and waist, flat-front skirt and full-box-pleated back with slightly longer length, dropped shoulders with set-in double-seamed sleeves, blue silk bias-cut trim at front, shoulders, sleeves and faux pockets trimmed with white buttons. And matching sleeveless vest with hook and eye closures.

27. WHITE WOOL FELT TOQUE
3" x 3 1/2" outside dimensions. 2 1/4" inside head width. White fur felt toque with narrowed upturned brim covered in ivory silk, wide double-folded ivory satin-silk banding, ivory silk moire bow and streamers, muslin lining, neck cord.

28. THREE COTTON ACCESSORIES
Comprises white fine muslin chemisette (4 1/2" shoulder width) with hand-finished edges, shaped collar with Valenciennes lace, draw-string ties; hankie (5" x 5") with fine hand-finished edge and drawn-work; sash or neck-scarf (33" L.) with hand-finished edges and scalloped V-shaped ends with petit-cut-work embroidery.

29. BENGALINE SILK THREE-PIECE ENSEMBLE WITH SOUTACHE BRAID
3 1/2" shoulder width. 7 1/2" waist. 7 1/4" skirt. Grey natural weave bengaline ensemble comprises full pleated skirt with intricately constructed box pleat at center back, matching fitted bodice with corded darts, V-shaped front waist, dropped shoulders with set-in double-seamed sleeves. With matching flared jacket, cording at collar and shoulders. Rich royal blue soutache trim on bodice, skirt, sleeves, jacket (faux soutache outlined pockets on jacket).

30. BLUE VELVET TOQUE IN WOODEN HAT BOX
2" x 2 3/4" exterior. 1 1/2" inside head width. Firm-shaped toque of ice-blue velvet has narrow brim at sides, wider brim at front and back, draped blue silk banding, silk floral trim, muslin lining. Original wooden hat box with delicately dotted paper lining, leather straps.

31. WOOL FELT TOQUE WITH BLUE SILK TRIM
2" - 2 1/2" outer size. 1" inside head width. Off-white fur felt toque with firm-shape has blue silk edging and underside, wider blue silk band with floral trim, fine muslin lining, black neck cord. Contained in original pale blue paper hat box with silk handle, original paper label "Alfred and Henry Rey/Caudry".

32. BEAVER TOQUE IN ORIGINAL HAT BOX
2 1/4" x 2 1/8". 1 1/2" inside head width. Light-grey beaver-fur toque with firm-rounded shape and very narrow brim has narrow grey silk bind, blue georgette banding and long veil or shawl, white feather, silver bird, muslin lining, original neck cord. Original cylindrical paper hat box with blue paper trim, and interior hat stand.

33. WOOL FLANNEL
MORNING COAT
4" shoulder width, 13" length. Of fine flannel wool blue and cream plaid with blue wool trim, cuffs and rolled collar. The morning coat has set-in sleeves, widely-flared shape, eight pearl buttons and blue cord tasseled ties.

34. TWILL SLIPPERS WITH
BLUE SILK RIBBONS
3". Narrow-width slippers of homespun twill have paper interiors and soles, ice-blue silk binding and bows, silver buckles, royal blue paper tips.

35. WOODEN AND
LEATHER BELLOWS
4 1/2". Wooden-framed bellows with circular carved design has brass hammered tip, leather bellows. A doll-sized bellows was offered by the Parisian doll boutiques of the 1860's.

36. GREEN LEATHER
SEWING NECESSAIRE
1 1/2" L. Firm-sided valise with rounded ends is covered with dark green leather, has incised decorative tooling, twill braided handles, silver petal-shaped clasp. Lid opens to reveal green and red paper lining and three miniature bone and gilt implements, plus miniature darning egg.

37. WATCH AND CHAIN
WITH FOB
4". Gilt tin faux-watch with Roman numeral face, hands fixed at 9 o'clock, has link chain terminating in belt loop with tiny turquoise bead.

38. PEWTER BED-WARMER
1 3/4" diam. Circular-shaped bed-warmer has top which unscrews to allow hot water. The doll-sized accessory is most unusual.

39. PATTERNED WOOL
SHORT JACKET
4 1/2" shoulder width, 5 1/2" L. Patterned brown and cream woven Vignone wool with unusual woven-in vertical band at front, loose shaping, set-in long sleeves, taupe silk neck banding, silver buttons over hook and thread closures.

40. LEATHER-COVERED
DOMED VALISE
3 1/2" L. Firm-sided leather valise with domed top is decorated with metal trim and bail handle; the early form of clasp involves insertion of pin through red leather loops. The valise has pale blue paper lining, red paper underside.

41. FELT TOQUE IN
WOODEN HAT BOX
3" x 2 1/2" exterior edges. 1 3/4" head-size width. Cream-colored and very soft fur felt toque with rounded top has narrow grosgrain ribbon binding, dark brown fur banding, fine muslin lining, original neck cord. Contained in original wooden hat box with lid, leather straps, green paper lining.

42. BROWN LEATHER ANKLE BOOTS
2 1/4" L. Soft dark brown kid ankle boots with scalloped top, flap closures with silver buttons, tiny heels, (one star-shaped decoration missing).

43. STRAW BONNET WITH
BROWN SILK RIBBONS
2 1/2" x 3". 1 3/4" interior opening. Straw bonnet for sitting primly atop the head, woven intricate design, brown silk grosgrain ribbon on brim and has ornately fashioned band with streamers, floral trim, silk lining, cord ties.

44. EARLY BONE-HANDLED MINIATURE JUMP-ROPE

16" L. Shaped bone handles are at each end of a tiny twill cord jump rope. The jump rope was one of the dozens of doll accessories available at doll shops during the era.

45. MINIATURE BONE OPERA GLASSES WITH STANHOPE IMAGE

1". Double-lens bone opera glasses have brass or gilt-metal frames, hanging hook, interior Stanhope image.

46. CAFE-AU-LAIT LINEN GOWN WITH CUTWORK TRIM

3 1/2" shoulder width. 8" waist. 8" skirt length. Brown linen gown with fitted bodice, flat-front skirt, set-in double-seamed sleeves, extended skirt back with bustle and back panel flaps, 2" knife-pleated hem flounce, hook and eye closure, elaborate decoration of baby rick-rack, braid and Teneriffe cutwork lace.

Mid-Century Costumes, 1855-1875.

47. THREE COTTON UNDERGAR-MENTS

Each of fine muslin, comprising square-necked shift (4 1/2" shoulder width) with set-in tucked short sleeves, unusual V-shaped set-in full-length side-darts; pantaloons (7 3/4" waist) with V-shaped front waist, gathered fullness, tucks at hemline; and petticoat (7 3/4" waist) with characteristic very full tiny gathers at the waistline allowing a very full hemline, draw-string waist.

48. FIVE PAIRS OF PANTALOONS

6"-10" waist, 6"-11" length. Each of white cotton with button or draw-string waist, cut for fullness of hips, with various tucks, embroidery or cut-work at lower legs, the drawstring pair with applied cord and Valenciennes lace.

49. RED WOOL KNIT UNDERGARMENTS AND LEATHER SLIPPERS

Including unusual short red wool petticoat (5" waist) with pinked-scalloped edging, catch-stitch embroidered circular embroidery, with attached red knit wool under-petticoat; 4 1/2" L. thick wool stockings with set-in foot, finishing edge at knee; 3" knit mitts or leg-warmers; and 2" narrow soft kid red slippers with ankle straps.

50. ORGANDY CHEMISETTE, SNOOD, TATTED COIFFE

Comprising sheer organdy chemisette (3" shoulder width) designed to be worn under jacket with bodice pleats, tatted collar interwoven with rose silk ribbons, ties at waist, with one matching sleeve; tatted coiffe (3" head piece, 17" overall) with interlaced rose silk ribbon; and delicately woven open-net snood with rose silk banding.

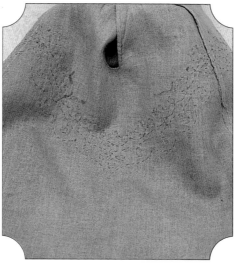

51. FITTED CORSET AND HOOP
6" waist. 7" hoop length. Included is tiny coutil corset with dart-shaped form enhanced by boning at center front and along the lacing holes, five pairs of lacing grommets, rose embroidery and rose grosgrain trim; and collapsible hoop with silk-covered wire hoops and brass hook and eye closure.

52. NATURAL LINEN GOWN WITH RED SOUTACHE TRIM
3 1/2" shoulder width. 10" waist. 13" overall length. One-piece gown of natural linen has square-cut bodice, short surplice sleeves, flat-front with shaped waist, full-length front panel with scalloped edging trimmed with tatting, set-in waist at sides and back with slightly gathered back waist, longer back skirt, button and loop closure. Tatting trim and elaborate red soutache trim, row of lingerie buttons.

Mid-Century Costumes, 1855-1875.

53. GRENADINE GOWN WITH ELBOW POUF SLEEVES
4" shoulder width. 9" waist. 10 1/2" skirt length. Delicately-woven cream grenadine gown with full muslin lining in bodice and skirt has fitted bodice with hook and eye closure at back, cording at waist and scooped neckline, elbow-length pouffed sleeves, box-pleated skirt, ruched ruffled trim at neckline, sleeves and hemline, lace trim inside neckline.

54. TWO WHITE DAY BONNETS
Each with about 2" inside head size. Includes cap of Broderie Anglaise with ruffled hand-made lace edging, magenta silk ribbons; and cap of reinforced Swiss batiste with ruffled lace edging interspersed with magenta ribbons.

55. HEELED BLUE LEATHER SHOES
2 3/4" L. Dark grey/blue soft kid slippers with high ankle backs, high-cut vamps decorated with gold-button rosette of self-material, tan kid unders, shapely black heels.

56. THREE COTTON UNDERGARMENTS
Comprising fine white muslin sacque with flared shape, pressed front pleats, sewn-down shaped collar, set-in sleeves, Swiss embroidery trim; white muslin petticoat with sewn-in V-shaped draw-string waist and double-ruffled hem flounce; and batiste pantaloons (7 1/2" waist) with fagoted Swiss embroidery and tucks.

57. FINE SILK GOWN WITH PAGODA SLEEVES
2 1/2" shoulder width. 5 3/4" waist. 8" skirt length. Fine cream silk gown with counterpane lavender print has fitted basque bodice with pagoda sleeves having wrist-length batiste liner, box-pleated skirt, violet silk ribbon band on skirt, purple delicate soutache braid on bodice, lace collar.

58. ORGANDY DAY BONNET
3" x 3 1/2" outside size. 2" inside head size. Of fine sheer organdy with handmade insertion lace and embroidery, ruffled edge with magenta velvet trim, mauve silk streamers.

59. BOMBE-SHAPED VELVET SEWING NECESSAIRE
2 1/2" L. Firm-sided, bombe-shaped valise has soft purple velvet covering with generous faux-leather decorative paper banding, hinged lid with tin medallion decorations, brass clasp, bound double handles. The red-paper-lined interior has tiny scissors and bone needlecase.

60. COTTON HANKIE AND COLLAR
Comprising hankie (3 1/2" square) with
delicately scalloped edging and embroidered
detail; and collar with pearl button closure,
cutwork and embroidered design, handworkship.

61. COTTON CHEMISE AND SILK STOCKINGS
Comprising fine white muslin chemise (5" shoulder width) with scooped-rounded
neckline, short gathered set-in sleeves, very delicate scallop-edged trim; and 5" L.
cream silk stockings with shaped foot and hand-stitched seam, woven pink rim.

62. LINSEY-WOOLSEY ENSEMBLE AND BONNET
3 1/2" shoulder width. 7" waist. 9" skirt length. Comprising skirt and jacket of
ivory and black counterpane, the full skirt with box pleats and vandyked trim of black
faille edged with purple silk ribbon, hook and eye waist closure; the bolero jacket
with dropped shoulders, vandyked trim to match skirt around the edge and sleeves,
cotton sateen lining. With Swiss batiste chemisette, rounded collar with scalloped
edge and embroidery. And bonnet of grey wool felt with black velvet band, muslin
lining, neck strings.

Mid-Century Costumes, 1855-1875.

23

63. FAILLE SILK SKIRT AND BASQUE JACKET
4" shoulder width. 8" waist. 8" skirt length. Pumpkin silk faille skirt has flat-front, pleated back with extended length, gathered flounce, hook and eye closure at side-front waist. With matching black silk faille basque jacket with hook and eye closures, black Cluny lace edging on jacket, Valenciennes lace at placket and cuffs. With pumpkin silk belt that hooks at the rear, having pumpkin silk gown edged in pumpkin/black banding.

64. WHITE WOVEN BONNET WITH BROWN VELVET TRIM
3" circular, 1 3/4" interior head opening. Unusual white woven bonnet with flat-top, brown velvet band and brim, the velvet extending to under-brim, brown silk ribbons, light-brown feathers, flowers, original delicate neck cord.

65. BLACK LEATHER FLAT BOOTS
2 1/2" L. Soft black kidskin boots have brown silk edging, four pairs of brass grommet laces, brown delicate laces with silver tips, brown silk ribbons with brass buckles, light-tan leather soles.

66. BROWN SUEDE GLOVES
2 1/2". Pair of brown soft suedeskin gloves have tiny scalloped wrist edging, over-cast stitching on fingers, set-in thumbs.

67. TAN KIDSKIN CLUTCH
1 3/4" L. Golden tan kidskin clutch with flap closure, leather belt loop, opens to reveal rich red leatherette interior with four compartments. The 130-year-old miniature purse is remarkably contemporary in its design and concept; it was designed to be used with a belt, resting upon one's hip.

68. SILK AND COTTON POPLIN ENSEMBLE
4" shoulder width. 8" waist. 8 3/4" skirt length. Comprising skirt and jacket of tiny brown/bronze silk and cotton poplin, the skirt of 1/2" pleats meeting at center front, wide black velvet waist, narrow black velvet trim at hemline; the bolero jacket with double row of trim around the edges and at cuffs, double-seamed sleeves. With batiste chemisette, lace-edged collar.

69. BLACK LEATHER ANKLE BOOTS
2" L. Soft black leather ankle boots have elastic V-shaped inserts, tan leather undersoles, tiny black shaped heels.

70. BLACK VELVET TOQUE
3" x 2", 2" inside opening. Soft black velvet toque has firm self-band, black velvet narrow ribbon streamers, peacock feather trim, brown net lining.

71. TAN KIDSKIN GLOVES
2 1/2" L. Soft kidskin gloves in light-tan color have scalloped edging at wrists, overcast stitched fingers, inset thumbs.

72. BLACK BEADED SHEER VEIL
8" x 8". Very delicate black English net veil is trimmed with tiny black beading in the manner of Point d'Esprit, silk chiffon ruched border.

Mid-Century Costumes, 1855-1875.

73. STRIPED MUSLIN MORNING DRESS
4" shoulder width. 14" overall length. Combed muslin morning or day dress has unusual pattern of very narrow slanted stripes separated by vertical white bands, V-shaped higher neckline edged with stand-up net trim, piping and frog closure of brown and candy-striped cord trim, pagoda sleeves with net trim, two pockets with cord trim, inverted pleat at back cascading into demi-train, self band at hemline.

74. BATISTE BLOUSE WITH BISHOP SLEEVES
5 1/2" shoulders, 6" L. to waist. Delicate white batiste blouse has draw-string neckline with scalloped edge, full bodice with draw-string waist, long sleeves, V-shaped overlay bodice and short sleeves with scalloped edging and delicate Swiss embroidery.

75. FOUR COTTON UNDERGARMENTS
Each about 4 1/2" shoulder width. Comprises Swiss batiste blouse with pin-pleats front and back, dart-shaped collar, set-in sleeves, crocheted lace trim; batiste chemisette or dickey, pin-pleated front and back, Dutch collar with beading, fagoting and Valenciennes lace trim; muslin draw-string petticoat with Swiss embroidery trim; muslin night sacque with V-shaped pleated yoke both front and back, set-in sleeves, eyelet embroidery.

76. TWO COTTON UNDERGARMENTS AND SNOOD
Each about 3" shoulder width. Comprises white lawn morning sacque with fitted collar, ruffled edging trimmed with Valenciennes lace, set-in curved sleeves, curved-dart shaping of back; fine muslin nightshirt with pin-tucked bodice, collar, cuffs and placket trimmed with tiny rick-rack and featherstitch. And finely-woven net hair-snood sized for about 17" (45 cm.) doll.

77. WHITE CAMBRIC GOWN
5" shoulder width. 10 1/2" belted waist. 16" full length. Heavy white woven cambric one-piece loose gown with tiny gathers at neckline, stand-up collar, open placket, dropped shoulders with elaborately constructed set-in detail, cartridge-pleated set-in sleeves with fitted draw-string cuffs, ribbon drawstring at throat, crocheted lace trim at collar, placket, belt edging, cuffs.

78. BLUE COTTON MUSLIN MORNING DRESS
3" shoulder width. 11" overall length. Heavily starched blue cotton poplin one-piece gown with woven vertical flowered bands has loose flared shape, trumpet sleeves with slight tuck and button near wrists, lace-edged collar and cuffs, extended train, faux double-breasted effect with one row of buttonholes.

79. THREE COTTON UNDERGAR-MENTS
Comprises fitted white batiste hip-length jacket (4" shoulder width) with dart-shaping and pleats both front and back, filet lace trim, armhole piping; batiste cotton nightshift (5" shoulder width, 14" L.) with pleated bodice, stand-up collar, set-in sleeves, cuffs, gathered back; batiste draw-string petticoat with stitched-down center darts at front center, daintiest hand-embroidery at hem.

Mid-Century Costumes, 1855-1875.

80. BLACK FAILLE FOUR-PIECE ENSEMBLE
3" shoulder width. 7" waist. 8 1/2" skirt length. Black matte faille skirt has flat front, full box-pleated back with extended train, 2 1/2" pleated flounce bordered by ruching, brown sateen lining, lace box-pleated trim at train. With fitted basque jacket having self-banding, full muslin lining, set-in sleeves with pleated cuffs. And extended length over-skirt with ruched detail at back, captured by hidden drawstrings. Included is batiste chemisette with crocheted collar.

81. IVORY SILK FAILLE BONNET
3" x 2" outside dimension. 1 3/4" inside head width. Ivory silk faille bonnet with wired frame and elaborately arranged fabric has silk binding decorated by tiny straw "petals", ivory silk banding and streamers, neck cord.

82. COUTIL CORSET AND CROCHETED HOOP
Comprising 4 1/2" white coutil corset with hand-stitching, intricately inset boning, hand-finished lacing holes, brass petticoat hook; and three-ring hoop (5" waist) with crocheted cover, hook and eye closure at waist.

83. COTTON NIGHTSHIFT AND SACQUE
Two garments, comprising fine muslin nightshirt with pintucking, lawn yoke with shirring, set-in sleeves, Valenciennes lace trim, pearl buttons (4" shoulder width, 11" length). And woven-stripe cotton sacque with flared shape, curved arms, diminutive eyelet trim, V-shaped tail (3 1/2" shoulder width, 5 3/4" length).

84. COUTIL FASHION CORSET

6" waist, 3" L. Elaborately constructed coutil corset with dart shaping, V-shaped bone inserts beside the brass lacing grommets, blue embroidered detail, blue grosgrain trim, cord laces.

85. TULLE DAISY-FLOWERED EUGENIE BONNET

3 1/2" x 5" outside size. 2 1/4" inside head size. Stiffened white tulle is arranged on wide oval frame, has ivory silk banding, upturned side with ivory silk bow, blue silk banding with lace detail and 12 fabric "daisies". Fabric bluettes and blue silk ribbons complete the decoration. Original neck cord.

86. PIQUE MORNING CAP WITH EMBROIDERY OUTLINE

2" inside head width. Designed to sit atop the head, the heavy pique cap has 1" box-pleated brim with tatting at edge, pique bow at front, pique bow and tails at back, blue silk ribbon trim, original cotton ties. A blue scrolled design is to serve as pattern for hand-embroidery.

87. BLUE SILK SNOOD

About 2" inside head width, with adjustable size. Beautifully woven ice-blue silk snood has blue silk streamers, original cord ties. Designed for use on 40-50 cm. (16-19 cm.) poupee.

88. BROWN VELVET
THREE-PIECE WALKING SUIT

2 1/2" shoulder width. 6 1/2" loosely fitted waist. 9 1/4" skirt length. Rich brown velvet three-piece suit has short fitted jacket with pagoda-style sleeves, faux-bustle, lace trim at cuffs, ice-blue silk edging and detail, lace trim at sleeves, full muslin lining; with matching skirt having demi-train, flat front, full back, 3" stiffening lining at hemline; and gathered overskirt with blue silk binding, elaborate 2 1/2" ice-blue silk ribbon sash at back with hook and eye closure and fringe.

89. BLACK VELVET
BONNET WITH FEATHER TRIM

2" inside head width. Firm-shaped black velvet bonnet folds in inside self-brim which is enhanced by ruched ivory silk, long ivory silk ties and bow, black feather trim, silk roses and leaves, stiffened gauze lining.

90. WIRED BLACK SILK BONNET

1 1/2" inside head width. Firmly-shaped wire-framed bonnet is so lavishly covered as to completely hide black silk. Tiny black beads with separating band of brown velvet decorate the inside rolled brim; wide black silk band, bow and streamers are decorated with large black feathers and tiny flowers, interior muslin lining and neck cord.

91. SILK POPLIN
THREE-PIECE WALKING SUIT
3 1/4" shoulder width. 7" waist. 8 3/4" skirt length. The ivory silk poplin ensemble has full skirt with flat front, bustle back with extended back, shirred front border with blue shantung vertical bands, blue shantung ruffle at back; with matching fitted jacket rounded in front, extended length in back with triple-tiered box pleats in alternate ivory and blue, set-in sleeves with vertical shantung banding over shirred ivory silk, blue turn-up cuffs, box-pleated collar at back, V-shaped collar front, blue stitched buttonholes. With uniquely constructed blue shantung over-skirt bordered by ruched ivory silk border, blue bows, hook and eye closure in front. The costume is remarkable for elaborate construction and decorative details.

92. BLACK TWILL
TRICORN BONNET
3" x 4" outside size. 2" inside head size designed to sit atop the head. Tricorn-shaped bonnet of black twill has upturned brim and is lavishly decorated with blue fabric flowers and black tulle. Black muslin lining, neck cord.

Mid-Century Costumes, 1855-1875.

93. BERRY-PRINT LINSEY WOOLSEY WALKING SUIT
3" shoulder width. 7" waist. 9" skirt length. Of cream linsey woolsey, the two-piece suit comprises long fitted basque jacket with double-banded front collar, box-pleated back collar, bustle-back with extended jacket tail, vandyked trim of apple-green silk, green silk bows; and full skirt with 4" gathered self-ruffle trimmed with green silk.

94. SWISS VOILE SACQUE AND CROCHET HOOP
3" shoulder width. 6" waist. 4 1/2" hoop length. Comprising hand-stitched fine Swiss voile sacque with double-seamed sleeves, delicate Swiss eyelet embroidery and trim on bodice and wide cuffs, three pearl buttons and hand-cut button holes. And crochet hoop with graduated size armature, collapsible shape, hook and eye closure.

95. MUSLIN PETTICOAT AND PANTALOONS WITH SOUTACHE TRIM
5" waist. 6" length. Comprising fine muslin petticoat with inverted box pleat front, cartridge pleated sides and back, tie-string waist, soutache trim at hemline. Matching pantaloons of shorter length with split-drawers, tie-string waist, soutache trim and scalloped leg borders.

96. WHITE COTTON CHEMISE, CHEMISETTE, CAP AND TIE
Suitable for 16"-18" doll. Comprising white batiste hand-stitched chemisette with bound seams and unusual hand-made rick-rack; white lawn chemise with delicate Swiss embroidery and tucks; muslin cap with lace trim and draw-string ties; and long batiste neck tie with cutwork and cast-scalloped-edge.

97. WHITE VOILE GOWN WITH OVERSKIRT AND UNDERGARMENTS
4" shoulder width. 7 1/2" waist. 10" skirt length. White voile gown has rounded neckline, bell sleeves, fitted waist, is richly trimmed with filet lace and satin silk ribbon. An overskirt at back of gown is attached by satin belt and appears as though it is actually part of the gown. Included is muslin chemise with single neck button and crocheted lace trim, inset V-shape sleeves, with pantaloons.

97A. WHITE DOTTED SWISS BONNET
About 2 1/2" face width. Heavily starched white dotted Swiss bonnet is hand-stitched, cording outlines the gathered inset at back of head, double band of blue silk ribbons are shadow-inset. There is a cluster of bobbinet trim around the face, decorated with blue silk ribbons and rosettes.

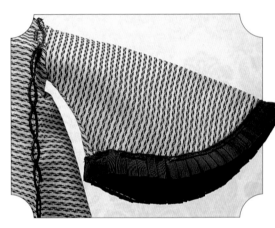

98. WOVEN COTTON DAY COAT
4 1/2" shoulder width. Flared cut jacket with rolled rounded collar has box-pleated black silk twill edging on collar, placket, hem and trumpet-shaped sleeves, five vertical rows of black soutache teardrop trim terminating in double scroll trim.

99. BLACK SILK TAFFETA BASQUE
4" shoulder width. 8 1/2" waist. 6" L. Fitted black taffeta silk basque has full brown cotton sateen lining, short puff banded sleeves, gathered flounce below the waist, red rick-rack trim, hidden hook and eye closure.

100. WHITE PIQUE SHORT JACKET
3 1/2" shoulder width. 8" length. White waffle-weave pique with brushed flannel underside forms a flared short jacket with set-in double-seamed fitted sleeves, demi-cuffs, stand-up back collar, single pocket, the back is fitted above the waist, with 14 box-pleats below. The jacket is trimmed with 1 1/2" Swiss eyelet trim, scalloped eyelet trim on collar, cuffs, pocket and along the front placket which hides the row of six lingerie buttons.

101. LINEN NURSING COSTUME
5" shoulder width. 14" overall length. Simple linen chemise-style gown with corded V-shaped bodice, self-banded neckline, double row of five full-length pleats, set-in sleeves with draw-string cuffs, pearl buttons, attached belt, embroidered red cross emblem. With matching linen apron, bib front with red cross, two large pockets with corded slit openings; and batiste headdress with stiffened brim and embroidered red cross.

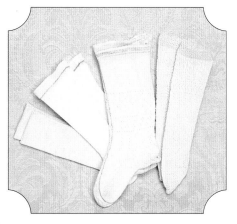

102. MUSLIN NURSING COSTUME
6" shoulder width. 15" overall length. White muslin chemise-style gown with set-in bodice, double row of three full-length pleats, gathered full sleeves with set-in cuffs, attached belt, embroidered red cross. With batiste apron, inverted V-shaped bodice to pin to uniform, large 4" wide pocket, string ties.

103. COTTON CHAMBRAY MORNING DRESS
3" shoulder width. 7" waist. 10" overall length. Blue and white striped cotton chambray one-piece dress has loose front with button-closure self-belt, set-in double-seamed sleeves, cuff bands, banding at collar and hem, 8 pearl buttons, back-fitted waist with box pleats, demi-train.

104. FOUR PAIRS OF COTTON KNIT STOCKINGS
4 1/2" L. to 6". White cotton knit stockings with woven or hand-stitched seaming and foot shape have various weave patterns, two with woven-in pink thread at knees.

105. BLACK SILK JACKET
WITH WATTEAU BACK

4 1/2" shoulder width. 10" waist. 15" length. Black silk jacket with very extended length is lined in brown cotton sateen except exposed lining of kimono-style sleeve with is lined with red silk, red featherstitch embroidery, seven red silk grosgrain bows.

106. GREY WOOL BASQUE WITH BUSTLE BACK

4 1/2" shoulder width. 10" width. 11" width. Charcoal wool basque with elongated drop has fitted waist, flat front, drop shoulders with set-in double-seamed sleeves, bustle back whose shape is achieved by interior drawstrings, 11 black bead buttons and hand-cast button holes, faux-rolled cuffs, wool middy braid trim outlines the jacket hem, neckline, cuffs and small pocket, red silk bow trim.

107. BLACK SILK FAILLE JACKET
AND STRAW BONNET

3 1/2" shoulder width. 8" length. A black silk faille jacket is deceptively simple, has dart-fitted back, flared sides, cape sleeves, hidden interior muslin waist ties, hook and tie closure under silk buttons. The jacket is elaborately trimmed with long black silk fringe at collar, sleeves, and hemline. And black straw woven bonnet with flat rounded top, flat brim, double row of red silk ribbons and rosette, black plume, muslin lining.

108. BLACK WOOL CAPE

3 1/2" shoulder width. Fine black wool has diamond-pointed center-seam back, dart-fitted neckline, triple rows of black cord, single button neck closure, 1" black spider-web tatting at hemline.

109. WHITE FUR MUFF AND STOLE

3" wide muff. 16" L. stole. Soft white fur muff has black fur tips, ivory silk twill padded lining, cord handle. With matching long stole with black fur tips, faux-fox-head with amber glass eyes, cord ties.

110. BLACK SILK FAILLE JACKET

4 1/2" shoulder width. 9" length. Black silk faille jacket with full flared cut has double-seamed sleeves, bias-cut back. The collar, open front, hemline, cuffs and sleeve-backs are edged with box-pleated ribbon trim of black silk with narrow silver band.

111. GREY LEATHER WRIST-LENGTH GLOVES AND FACE VEIL

2" L. gloves. Of soft grey kidskin, the gloves are stitched with pale rose thread, separate thumbs, ivory kidskin binding and covered buttons of faux snaps. And veil of very fine English net with delicately-woven edge, draw-string closure.

112. OLIVE-GREEN TWILL HOODED COAT
4 1/2" shoulder width. 16" length. Olive-green twill paletot with single box pleat at back has two large pockets with gathered tops, double-seamed sleeves, hood with draw-string gathers, black silk facing, six buttons.

113. BROWN WOOL FELT GAITERS
3" L. Sized for fit to poupee or fashion doll, the brown wool felt gaiters have shaped ankles, three silver button closures, red trim along all edges, red leather foot straps with silver buckles.

114. GREY WOOL FLANNEL PATTI SACQUE
4 1/2" shoulder width. 8 1/2" length. Smoke-grey wool flannel short jacket has widely flared sides, decorative collar, two pockets, very wide set-in double-seamed sleeves, purple silk binding at all edges, double row of silver buttons, single row of buttonholes. The color combination was particular to the early 1860 era, yet very popular at that time.

115. MIDNIGHT-BLUE WOOL FELT PATTI SACQUE
4 1/2" shoulder width. 7 1/2" length. Of heavy wool felt, the flared short jacket has open pleats at back and sides, rolled stand-up collar, set-in double-seamed sleeves, faux-double-breasted effect with double row of brass buttons (yet single row of buttonholes), two faux-pocket flaps. The jacket is entirely edged in narrow black silk ribbon, has brass buttons on flaps, cuffs and edging the open pleats at back and sides.

116. WOOL TWEED WALKING SUIT

3 1/2" shoulder width. 9" waist. 11" skirt length. Brown wool tweed suit with mustard-gold flecks comprises jacket of nearly-full-length with fitted bodice and waist, flat front, Princess-style flap back, rolled cuffs of double-seamed set-in sleeves, dropped shoulders; and matching skirt with flat-front, and very full extended back. The seams are trimmed with yellow cord, and a faux pocket with mustard silk ribbon tabs; 13 silk-covered buttons.

117. ZEPHYR WOOL PLAID WALKING SUIT
5 3/4" shoulder width. 11" waist. 11 3/4" skirt length. Blue and ivory plaid lightweight wool suit comprises long jacket with fitted bodice, jacket sides flaring over skirt, fullness to back of jacket captured by hidden drawstrings, dropped shoulders, set-in sleeves, brown cotton sateen lining, black glass bead buttons, hand-cast buttonholes, pockets edged in black velvet, full skirt, black velvet banding on skirt, jacket, sleeves, lace collar trim.

118. SILK BROADCLOTH GOWN WITH BLUE VELVET TRIM
4" shoulder width. 9" waist. 14 3/4" overall length. One-piece gown of bronze-colored silk broadcloth with narrowest blue woven stripe has fitted waist, front bodice that flaps over the left shoulder, trumpet sleeves, fitted back with extended train decorated with attached gathered faux-train. Blue velvet banding the decorated the hemline, faux train, sleeves, collar and entire front center. There is lingerie lace trim at the neckline, sleeves and front, full cotton sateen lining.

119. WOOL FLANNEL GOWN WITH JACKET FRONT
5" shoulder width. 19" length. Grey wool flannel jacket dress has princess lines, attached jacket with long sleeves, brown cotton sateen lining, blue quilted collar, cuffs and pocket flaps, blue silk cording at hemline and edge of jacket, elaborate lace jabot and cuff trim, two pockets, blue silk ribbon bow trim, fitted back with box pleats, blue silk ribbon streamers.

120. FOUR-PIECE LINGERIE ENSEMBLE
4" shoulders. 6" waist. 9" front skirt length. Comprising muslin chemise with lace-trimmed front panel, lace at collar and short sleeves; matching pantaloons with lace trim; batiste petticoat with flat front, gathered back, wide ruffle with box pleats at sides and back, demi-train; lawn outer petticoat with lace-trimmed dust ruffle in front, two rows of dust ruffles at back, demi-train, tie-string waist.

121. THREE UNDERGARMENTS
About 6" waist. Comprising white cotton hand-hemmed drawers with button and draw-string ties; white cotton summer stays, hand-stitched, with delicate bone inserts in intricate pattern, hand-edged lacing holes; and white muslin petticoat with draw-string waist, double row of hem ruffles.

122. PRINTED VOILE DAY DRESS AND PINAFORE

4" shoulder width. 8" waist. 10 3/4" skirt length. Delicate lavender petals are printed on white voile background, the set comprises dress with fitted waist, gathered full bodice, 1" wide gathered collar, set-in long sleeves with double seams, gathered ruffles at cuffs partially hiding hands, button back, flared skirt, 4" dust ruffle, trimmed with filet lace. With pinafore skirt having apron front with graduated-length dust ruffle, waist band with button back, wide bands from side of apron tie in the back in large ornamental/functional bows.

123. ROYAL PURPLE SILK TURBAN AND BELT SASH

2 1/2" circ. outside dimension of turban. 2" inside width for head. 9" length of sash. Multi-patterned purple and ivory silk turban with firm-sided brim is decorated with self-silk bow, purple velour pom-pom, unusual colorful silk "splash", has muslin lining and neck cord. And purple silk taffeta belt sash of 2 1/2" W. banded ribbon with stitched wide bow and hook for attaching to back waist. The sash is contained in original Parisian boutique box.

124. WHITE MULL GOWN WITH SILK RIBBON TRIM
6 1/2" shoulder width. 16 1/2" overall length. One-piece gown for larger early bebe of white sheer mull with princess style, dart-shaping, front hooks and loops, is trimmed with triple banding of delicate blue silk ribbon, Valenciennes lace, blue bows of grosgrain ribbon, white piping at each back seamline, bustle back and two side-seam pockets, each trimmed with six bands of narrow blue ribbon. Designed to be worn over underliner chemise, probably of same blue as trim.

125. FINE MUSLIN FLOWERED PRINT ENSEMBLE
3 1/2" shoulder width. 8" width. 9 1/2" skirt length. Three-piece ensemble with delicate blue and red flower print comprises fitted long jacket with fold-over cuffs and five pearl buttons; full skirt; and pannier-styled overskirt, each trimmed with delicate Swiss embroidery.

126. WHITE PIQUE PRINCESS-STYLE SUIT
4 1/2" shoulder width. 9" waist. 9 1/2" skirt length. Of heavy white pique comprising jacket with fitted bodice, dropped shoulders, set-in cornet sleeves; and matching skirt with hidden placket opening and box-pleats at front, cartridge pleating on back full skirt. The suit is decorated with white braid and cord trim in elaborate garlands, has pique covered buttons on skirt and jacket, corded neckline, sleeve edges and hem.

127. BATISTE GOWN WITH TRAIN
4" shoulder width. 12" front length. 22" back length. Batiste white princess-styled gown has 2" wide insert of jabot-styled lace forming the collar and extending down the entire front covering the pearl button closures, elbow-length sleeves extended by 2" length of alternating Valenciennes and Swiss eyelet lace, two lace and Swiss eyelet pockets, double row of lace and Swiss eyelet at hemline extending into long train.

128. TWO PETTICOATS AND SUMMER SKIRT
Each about 7" waist. Comprises batiste petticoat with flat front, 4" dust ruffle with lace trim, extended dust ruffle trim; muslin petticoat with bustle back, Swiss eyelet embroidery; and full gathered grenadine skirt over gauze underskirt, picot-edged silk ribbon trim to match.

129. IVORY COTTON SATEEN TWO-PIECE ENSEMBLE

4 1/2" shoulder width. 7" waist. 11 1/2" skirt length. Ivory cotton sateen ensemble comprises muslin-lined fitted jacket with extended box-pleat tails, rolled collar with stand-up Alencon lace inside collar and 1" band of lace below the collar, set-in sleeves with elbow darts, pearl button closure, lace trim at cuffs and lower jacket edge. With elaborately constructed net-lined skirt having draped folds, and knife-pleated trim alternating with gathers, three bands of Alencon lace, double bustle and demi-train.

130. BRONZED LEATHER BOOTS "MODES DE PARIS"

1 3/4" L. Brown leather high laced boots with metallic "bronzed" finish have gracefully shaped tops with overcast edging, brass grommets, original lacing, leather and silver buckle decoration, tan leather soles, tiny black heels. Marked "Modes de Paris" in oval with initials A.P. and incised number 45 (indicating centimeter size of doll for which the boots were designed.

131. WHITE WOOL FLANNEL PLUSH BONNET AND SILK GLOVES

3 1/2" diameter, outer size. 1 1/2" interior head width. Of brushed white wool flannel plush, the bonnet has wire-framed brim, ivory silk band, bow and ties, muslin lining, and is contained in original small wooden hat box with green paper lining, leather straps. And 4" silk evening gloves with set-in gloves and 1" woven border.

132. IVORY COTTON SATEEN ENSEMBLE AND UNDERGARMENTS
3 1/2" shoulder width. 8" waist. 11" length. Comprising fitted jacket with jabot-style lace placket, elaborately arranged lace at collar and hemline, muslin lining, hook and eye closure; with very elaborately constructed skirt of alternating bands of lace and box pleats at front, triple hoop-framed bustle at rear, train trimmed with lace and sateen pleated fans, gauze lining. With matching muslin drawers and petticoat with train, lace trim.

133. BLACK LEATHER ANKLE BOOTS SIGNED C.C.
2" L. Black kid leather ankle boots with leather and buckle trim, brass grommets, original lacing, tan leather soles signed C.C. and 4. (one with original paper label).

134. GARNET SILK SATIN TWO-PIECE FASHION ENSEMBLE WITH TRAIN
3" shoulder width. 7 1/4" waist. 9" skirt length. A fitted garnet silk satin hip-length jacket has ivory silk plastron and bodice, set-in sleeves, flowered silk banding at cuffs, lace trim, gauze lining, with matching skirt fitted closely to body shape at front and sides, then gathered into exaggerated pouf at the rear, decorated with horizontal pleated bands of floral-printed silk, trimmed with maroon silk bows, pleated skirt flounce extends all around train, lace trim, muslin dust ruffle on train. Included is original muslin chemise.

135. RED LEATHER PURSE AND FAUX-MUFF
Comprising 2" W. red leather expandable purse with red muslin accordion-shaped interior, silver buckle and clasp, silver link chair. And firm-shaped circular faux-muff with sealed padded magenta silk hand-rests, magenta silk tassels and cord.

135A. RED KIDSKIN FLAT SHOES
2 1/4" L. Soft red kid leather slippers are side-stitched, has high cut rounded vamps trimmed with red leather wings and silver buckle, tan leather soles marked "4".

136. WOVEN RED SNOOD
About 2 1/2" width. Designed for wear on 17"-20" poupee, the snood is loosely-woven pale russet silk cords which draw to desired size by black interwoven thread and red silk ribbons.

137. THREE FASHION DOLL ACCESSORIES
Comprising 1 1/4" glass perfume bottle with silver fretwork overlay, turquoise lid; 14-blade 1 1/2" bone fan with fretwork design, interwoven silk ribbon, folds and opens; and 1 1/2" blown glass cologne bottle with stopper, pontil base.

138. IVORY SILK SATIN GOWN
3 1/2" shoulder width. 13" overall length. One-piece ivory satin gown in loosely dart-fitted Princess style with flared skirt has V-shaped neck trimmed with box-pleated cerise silk bands and lace insertion, matching bands attached in curving waves, four rose silk bows, hook and eye closure, inverted box pleats at back demi-train.

139. TWO UNDERGARMENTS FOR POUPEE
5" waist. Comprising coutil corset with red banding, red stitching, boning, brass lacing grommets at back, hook and eye closure at front. And hand-stitched drawers of white muslin with tucks and Swiss embroidery at legs, drawstring waist.

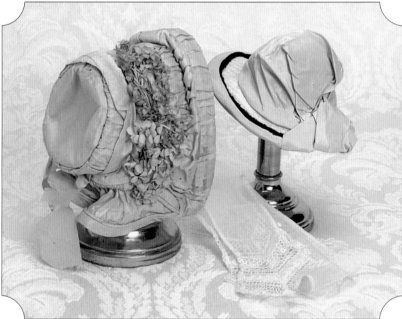

140. SILK FASHION CORSET AND MUSLIN CRINOLINE
5" waist. Comprising silk satin laced corset with bone insets, muslin lining, laced back, blue silk and lace trim, shaped waist; and muslin crinoline with three graduated circumference hoop inserts, drawstring waist.

141. WHITE FUR MUFF IN ORIGINAL BOX
3" width. Lush white fur padded muff is decorated with pale blue silk cords and tassels, is contained in original glass-lidded box with original price label.

142. AQUA SILK CALASH BONNET
1 1/2" - 2" inside head width. Elaborately arranged aqua silk taffeta is arranged over straw and wire-frame form, the sides drawn over the ears and hiding the face, decorated with tiny fabric lilacs, aqua silk ribbons.

143. AQUA SILK BONNET AND LACE SCARF
Suitable for fashion doll about 17". A bonnet designed to sit atop the head is shaped of woven straw and wire, has gathered pouf of silk on top that tucks under the brim which is covered by same silk and black velvet. Silk lined, black ties. And 14" fine batiste neck scarf is trimmed with three alternate bands of lace and embroidery, has hand-stitched edging.

Mid-Century Costumes

144. SWISS BATISTE ENSEMBLE WITH UNDERGARMENTS

2 1/2" shoulder width. 8" waist. 8" skirt length. Comprising muslin-lined long-fitted batiste jacket with double row of buttons (one side with working buttonholes, princess-seamed back, lace trim at neckline and front, green silk bows; batiste flat-front skirt with gathered dust ruffle, demi-train; batiste overskirt which attaches with wide batiste bow at rear and is decorated with green taffeta bows. Included are five undergarments: lawn drawstring petticoat, muslin petticoat, muslin underslip with tucks; muslin drawers with tucks and Swiss embroidery, muslin chemise with Valenciennes lace.

**145. LINSEY WOOLSEY
ENSEMBLE WITH TRAIN**
3 1/2" shoulder width. 8" waist. 9" skirt length.
Ensemble comprises fitted jacket with set-in
sleeves, V-shaped neckline, ivory piping, chiffon
ruched neck decoration, fringed cuffs.
elaborately constructed back with ruching, silk
bows. With extremely elaborate skirt having six
rows of ruching at hemline and fringed edging,
tightly fitted gathered skirt over hips, elaborately
arranged bustle and train; ivory silk bows down
the entire front. Included is velvet turban hat
with folded green and mauve velvet ribbons,
wire frame, net lining.

**146. ROSE SILK GLOVES
AND FEATHER MUFF**
4" L. gloves. Elbow-length gloves of rose silk
have set-in thumbs. With real feather muff and
padded silk lining.

147. AUBERGINE TAFFETA SKIRT
9 1/2" waist. 8" length. Crisp aubergine taffeta skirt has flat front, wide flared sides, very full back with demi-train, has pressed pleat horizontal bands at front, gathered 1 1/2" taffeta bands at rear with pinked edges, hook and eye closure.

148. FRENCH FASHION ENSEMBLE
4" shoulder width. 8" waist. 10" skirt length. Comprising ivory wool basque with four pearl buttons, rounded neckline, set-in double-seamed sleeves, fitted back with corded trim, lavender banding and tatted trim, hook and eye closures; with grey silk taffeta princess-style skirt, gathered dust ruffle, box-pleated back with bustle drawstrings, demi-train.

149. IVORY CASHMERE CAPELET
About 3 1/2" shoulder width. 8" length. Ivory cashmere cape has ivory satin lining, box-pleated lined hood, ivory satin piping at neckline, 1 1/2" border of scalloped Lille lace.

150. IVORY SILK FAILLE GOWN WITH CLUNY LACE
3" shoulder width. 8" waist. 12" overall length. Heavy ivory silk twill or Petersham is constructed with horizontal cut, modified Princess style with extended-length box-pleated back, set-in elbow-length sleeves, tiny ruched banner at front hemline, ivory silk streamers, Cluny lace, Valenciennes lace at hemline.

151. POLISHED COTTON GOWN

4 1/2" shoulder width, 7" waist, 13" overall length. Princess styled one piece gown of lavendar plaid has set-in sleeves, box pleats at back with extended length, sew-in darts at elbows to emphasize widened cuffs, rounded neckline with lace trim, black velvet banding and bows overall, muslin lined bodice, hook and eye closure.

152. POINT D'ESPRIT SCARF

3 1/2" width. 61" length. Fine delicate point d'esprit lace with guipure lace tips at either end.

153. STRIPED COTTON BLOUSE

4 1/4 shoulder width. 8" waist. Striped red and white cotton blouse has fitted waist, wide pleats at front, rolled stand-up collar, set-in bishop sleeves, fitted pique cuffs, inset back bodice.

154. BRODERIE ANGLAISE AND LACE COLLAR AND CUFFS

8" neck opening. Rounded collar and 3" L. cuffs are elaborately constructed of alternate vertical bands of broderie Anglaise with fagoting and Gros Point de Venise lace, the bands separated by hand-stitched cording. Maroon silk ribbons decorate the closures.

155. FINE LINEN GOWN AND JACKET IN REVIVAL EMPIRE STYLE

5" shoulder width. 15" overall length. A loosely-fitting fine white linen gown has square yoke, trumpet sleeves, empire waist, and full gauze lining. The matching jacket has tasseled cord ties at front. Both pieces are decorated with elaborate French knotted design, ruffled borders and white glass buttons.

156. ROSE SILK SATIN GOWN, PEARLS AND STOCKINGS
2 1/2" shoulder width. 5" waist. 7" skirt length. Rose satin gown has V-shaped fitted waist with cord-trim, triple V-shaped darts, laced back, extended Bourdon lace collarette, short lace demi-sleeve with Bourdon lace trim, very full box-pleated skirt with lace trim. Included are pearl necklace and bracelet; woven cotton stockings to match.

157. WHITE WOVEN STRAW BONNET
3" x 2 1/2" outer size. 1 1/2" inside head width. Circular woven white straw bonnet designed to sit atop the head is decorated with elaborately arranged mauve silk grosgrain ribbon, has muslin lining and original ties.

158. BLACK HEELED ANKLE BOOTS SIGNED B.V.
1 3/4" L. Of soft black kid leather banded with very narrow brown silk ribbon, the ankle boots have brown leather soles, 1/2" heels, three-button flap closures, are signed B.V. (in rectangle).

159. ROSE SILK SATIN BONNET
3" x 2 1/2" outer size. 1 1/2" inside head width. The seemingly soft shape of the rose silk satin bonnet is maintained by the hidden wire and buckram frame. There is a pale rose silk band with rosette trim.

160. BONE DRESSER SET IN ORIGINAL BOX
5 1/2" x 2 1/2" box. 2" L. hand mirror. Within a padded rose silk-lined box are arranged bone toiletry objects sized for display with poupee dolls about 17"-20". Comprising styling comb, swansdown puff, small lidded jar, bristle brush, and mirror.

161. WHITE BATISTE BEBE FROCK WITH BUSTLE AND TRAIN
5" shoulder width. 13 1/2" overall length. One-piece jacket dress has stand-up collar with double row of picot lace, long set-in sleeves with 2" embroidered faux cuffs and double row of picot lace, placket trimmed with horizontal tucks and triple row of picot lace which extends over hips and is covered by faux-jacket trimmed with inset and edging of Swiss embroidery. The attached skirt has vertical bands of tucking and Swiss embroidery trim above the pleated dust ruffle. At the back is a draw-string bustle below narrow pleats and an extended train trimmed with double row of Swiss embroidery.

162. WHITE COTTON FROCK WITH UNDERSLIP
4" shoulder width. 8" waist. 8 3/4" skirt length. One-piece white lawn gown has pouf sleeves, inset panel at bodice with scalloped edging and embroidered detail, unusual collar detail with wide wings which extend over both sleeves and terminate in long lappets in the front, rounded collar in back, fitted waist, cartridge pleated skirt with hook and eye closure, hand-embroidered detail. And matching muslin slip with scalloped detail at bodice, hem and short sleeves, drawstring neckline and waist.

163. WOVEN STRAW TODDLER'S "WALKING" HAT
5 1/2" x 6" outer dimensions. 4" inside head width. Circular woven strap bonnet in upside down basket shape is bound with blue muslin, decorated with criss-cross of blue velvet banding, blue velvet fringe, lined with gauze. The firm-sided hat was designed to protect a young baby's head when first learning to walk. Introduced to France during the 1850's, the style is unique to that era; it is found on early Steiner bebes as well as paper mache taufling babies and automatons from 1850 to about 1875.

164. BLUE LEATHER LACED BOOTS WITH SUNBURST PATTERN
3 1/2" L. Soft kid leather boots dyed royal blue have stitched front, seven pairs of brass lacing grommets, superbly formed soles and heels in the manner of earlier Huret-type poupee shoes, original blue laces with brass tips. The blue leather is decorated with gold "sunburst" design.

165. PAIR, EARLY KNITWEAR WOOL BOOTIES
3" foot length. Lightweight white wool in open weave lacy pattern has tighter, "warmer", pattern on soles, is decorated with interwoven blue designs, has blue wool cord ties with white wool pompom tips.

166. WHITE BOOK LINEN FROCK AND BONNET FOR MIGNONETTE
1 1/4" shoulder width. 4" overall length. The flared-side princess-style frock is hand-stitched, has cording at edges, four rows of tiny silk buttons, decorative bands of tatting, ruffled lace, box-pleated Swiss embroidery in tiny pattern. With matching Valenciennces lace and Swiss embroidery bonnet trimmed with ivory silk ribbons.

167. WHITE PIQUE FROCK
6 1/2" shoulder width. 18" high waist. 12" skirt length. Horizontally ribbed white pique frock has fitted bodice with high waist, short capelet sleeves, rounded neckline, wide front panel which extends into large box pleats around the sides and back.The front panel is richly embellished with soutache braid and trim. A separate matching sash attached at the back forming a large bow with three small lappets and two longer lappets.

168. WHITE PIQUE FROCK
3 1/2" shoulder width. 10" waist. 6" skirt length. Horizontally ribbed white pique one-piece frock has vertically tucked bodice, square-cut neckline and short sleeves with cutwork and tatted trim, fitted waist, box-pleated back of skirt. The front panel of dress wraps to the side with tiny hidden pearl buttons and loops.

169. SILK TRI-COLOR BONNET
6" circular shape. The bonnet, of elaborately arranged padded folds in bronze silk-satin, is bound with stiffened and draped maroon silk satin, edged with box-pleated lace and trimmed with large burgundy taffeta bow trimmed with brass ormulu buckle, is completely padded on the interior to allow the hat to perch directly atop the head.

170. BROWN LEATHER SHOES WITH ROSETTES
4 3/4" L. Of very soft crushed black kid-leather, the shoes are supported by tacked-on hard leather soles in the Huret-style. Narrow brown silk ribbons bind the edges and a ruffled brown silk hand-tied rosette is decoration. The shoe is an early model of the classic Jumeau shoe that appeared some two decades later.

Costumes, Bonnets, Shoes And Accessories, 1875-1890

170A. WHITE PIQUE BEBE FROCK
5" shoulder width. 14" waist. 13" overall
length. One-piece frock of horizontally
ribbed pique is constructed to fit tightly to
bebe child-like body, has slant-cut front
panel which folds across the bodice and
attached by button and loop, dropped
shoulders with set-in double-seamed
sleeves, cording at shoulder seams, Swiss
embroidery, braid and lace edge the neck
line, cuffs, front, and pocket. The shaped
back has box pleats below the hips edged
with braid.

**171. TODDLER'S WOVEN STRAW
"WALKING" HAT**
5" x 6" outer dimensions. 4" inside head
width. A variation of #163, this example
has open-weave lacy pattern on top, is
decorated with draped brown velvet band
and bow. The firm sides of the hat protected
the baby's soft cranium during tumbles
while learning to walk.

**172. EMBROIDERED LINEN
SLIPPERS**
4 1/2" L. Natural brown linen slippers with
firm-edged quilted linen soles has white
corded edging, embroidered floral and vine
decoration.

172A. WOVEN STRAW BONNET WITH BROWN VELVET TRIM
8" x 10" outer size. 5" inside head width. Loosely-woven brown stiffened straw forms the shape of the elaborately trimmed bonnet designed to perch atop the head, with wire-strengthened brown velvet-covered brim and ties, bronze grosgrain silk ribbon trim, arrangement of fabric leaves and flowers. Black cotton sateen lining.

173. ROYAL PURPLE COAT WITH CREWEL EMBROIDERY
10" shoulder width. 20" overall length. Rich royal purple velvet coat has striped silk lining, large rounded collar with shoulder cut-outs, dropped shoulders, long sleeves. The coat is richly crewel embroidered in classic floral and leaf pattern in shades of ivory and blue.

174. BROWN LEATHER SHOES WITH NAILED SOLES
4 1/2" L. Thick brown leather shoes with separately cut and stitched fronts, have heart-shaped vamp, original brown grosgrain ties, thick leather soles and heels firmly tacked to uppers with a border of tiny brass nails. Incised "18".

175. RED WOOL CHILD'S DRESS
10" shoulder width. 22" overall length. Red worsted wool princess-style dress with loosely fitted flared shape has round collar trimmed with Swiss embroidery, dropped shoulders with set-in double-seamed sleeves, cording at shoulder seam, black soutache trim in scrolled designs, red cotton sateen lining, box pleats at extended back, back detachable waist belt with soutache trim.

176. SCOTTISH PLAID WORSTED WOOL FROCK
5 1/2" shoulder width. 19" waist. 15" floor-length skirt. Red and black plaid-checkered woven worsted wool frock with shaded detail of print, has bias-cut yoke to enhance the pattern, gathered and pleated lower bodice, set-in waist, modified gigot double-seamed sleeves, flat-front skirt, box-pleats at extended-length back, red cotton sateen lining on skirt, cotton muslin lining of bodice, hook and eye closure. Interest in Scottish costume had a long tradition in France; the bebe costume is unusual for its full length rather than the "new" child length of skirt.

177. BLACK CHALLIS WOOL BONNET
7" x 5" outer size. 4" inside head width. Wire-shaped bonnet designed to sit on the back of head, is trimmed with elaborately folded fabric, large bow with tucks surmounted by box-pleated headdress, long black grosgrain ribbons, black muslin lining.

Costumes, Bonnets, Shoes And Accessories, 1875-1890

178. EARLY DAMASSE FROCK WITH CUTWORK YOKE
5 1/2" shoulder width. 16" waist. 11" skirt length. Bebe frock has delicately worked cutwork bodice with scallop-shaped neckline, fluted cap sleeves with scalloped edge, button and loop closure, damasse-type cotton skirt with unusual woven pattern, insertion of eyelet at hem, silk ribbon sash with cutwork loops.

179. WHITE COTTON DAMASSE BEBE DRESS
5" shoulder width. 14" waist. 9 1/2" skirt length. The one-piece damasse frock has rounded neckline with overcast tiny scalloped edging, low V-shaped bodice with embroidered detail, dropped shoulders with cording at shoulder seams, puffed sleeves with scalloped edging, set-in waist with draw-string ties, cartridge pleated very full skirt.

180. STRIPED WIRED COTTON BONNET
6 1/2" x 6" outer dimension. 4" inside head width. Cotton bonnet in printed pattern of narrow blue and ivory stripes is gathered at back of head, the face framed by deep five-wire-framed brim which is decorated with self-fabric bows on the outside, and rose silk loops on the interior.

181. FOUR PAIRS OF EARLY STOCKINGS
To fit foot about 2 - 2 1/2". 4" L. With shaped feet and hand-stitched seams, comprising two matching blue pairs with white catch-stitch design; one lavender pair in similar design; one striped claret/ivory pair with set-in feet.

182. WHITE PIQUE FROCK WITH SOUTACHE TRIM
8" shoulder width. 22" overall length. Horizontally ribbed white pique loosely-draped frock has square-cut yoke with full-length separate front panel, hook and eye closures to side panel in jacket-lie effect, flared sides, crest-shaped pockets, demi sleeves, princess seaming in back with fanny box pleats hidden by elaborately folded sash. The costume is decorated with soutache in floral pattern and Cluny lace.

183. WHITE PIQUE JACKET DRESS
8" shoulder width. 22" overall length. Horizontally ribbed white pique jacket dress has panel front with pearl button closure, two large pockets, long sleeves, sailor collar with 3" drop at back, princess-style back with knife pleats and wide hip belt. The costume is decorated at collar, cuffs, hem, front panels, sash, and pockets with 1" wide Paraquay knotted lace.

184. WHITE WAFFLE-WEAVE BONNET
6" x 13" outside dimensions. 4" inside head width. Thick waffle-weave cotton pique with flannel lining has box pleats framing the face, surmounted by double row of scallops and pleats in same fabric, 1 1/2" wide waffle weave bows at top and back of head, draw-string at neck, 6" attached capelet, trimmed with braid and delicate scallop-edged trim.

185. WHITE COTTON BONNET
6" x 13" outside dimensions. 4" inside head width. Fine white cotton bonnet is shaped by wide box pleats captured by two graduated width borders of Swiss embroidery, lace cluster at forehead and silk ivory ribbons, 4" attached capelet with Swiss embroidery edging and soutache trim, woven medallion of soutache trim at back of head.

186. SILK AND COTTON BEBE FROCK WITH BONNET AND SLIPPERS
6 1/2" shoulder width. 22" length. Comprising white lawn frock lined with nainsook, lace insertion panel on front with alternate bands of ivory silk ribbon, puffed sleeves, stand-up collar, loosely draped front, defined waist and pin-tucked bodice in back, 2"-3" Lille lace trim borders the front panel, hem and cuffs. And ivory grosgrain bonnet with box-pleat shaping, lavish cluster lace and silk ribbons at crown, 3" drape at neck, bands of lace at back and bottom edge, muslin lining with internal drawstring. And ivory silk booties with muslin lining, ankle straps, fringed trim, silk ribbon ties.

187. FLOCKED TENERIFFE LACE CAPELET COAT AND SILK ORGANZA BONNET

5 1/2" shoulder width. 18" overall length. White jacket dress has teneriffe lace bodice, lower skirt and hip-length cape with scalloped edging, midriff and set-in sleeves of flocked pique, white cording at seams, rolled cuffs. The long capelet hides the fully constructed jacket-dress below. And black silk organza wired bonnet with tucked brim, black velvet band and wired bow, black boa feather, white silk organza lining.

188. WHITE BATISTE DRESS WITH BRODERIE ANGLAISE

7" shoulder width. 16" waist. 13" length. Delicate white lawn frock has gathered yoke, intricately constructed bodice of alternate bands of eyelet and tucks flanked by scalloped broderie anglaise, set-in sleeves with gigoting above alternate bands of tucks and eyelet, stand-up eyelet collar, set-in waist with cording, gathered waist with 7" of broderie anglaise. The collar and shoulder seams are covered by featherstitch.

190. TIERED LACE BONNET WITH PLEATED BRIM

6" x 4" outside dimensions. 3" inside head width. Delicate bonnet of ivory tulle covered with triple ruffled tiers, medallion center, thickly clustered lace in box pleats frames the face and is decorated with ivory and maroon silk ribbons, ivory silk ribbon ties, draw-string to back of head allows for size adjustment.

189. WHITE WOOL BONNET

9" x 7" outside dimensions. 3" inside head width. White wool bonnet has wire-shaping at brim and back of head, ruched detail around the face, gathered back with ruched medallion at back of head, double bavolet of graduated lengths with pinked edges, double brim of graduated lengths, pinked edges, ivory silk ribbons.

191. IVORY LACE AND MAROON SILK BONNET
8" x 7" outside dimensions. 5" inside head width. Elaborately constructed all-lace bonnet with padded silk lining has bands of lace trimmed with same ruffled lace, inserted Swiss eyelet darts, gathered lace ruffle frames the face, double ruffle at crest with ornately arranged maroon grosgrain silk ribbon and bows around the entire bonnet and as ties.

192. WHITE PIQUE FROCK WITH TIERED PLEATS
7" shoulder width. 23" overall length. Vertically ribbed white pique with princess styling has 2 1/2" bands of pleats at yoke, suspender-style down the front and back, as demi-sleeves and as multi-layered skirt. Delicate lace edges each of the bands, 12 fabric-covered buttons.

193. WHITE PIQUE JACKET DRESS
7" shoulder width. 20" overall length. Horizontally ribbed pique jacket dress has drop waist, jacket front with inset eyelet bands and scalloped edging, overlapping 4" border of box pleats, the overlapping border is splayed in rear to enhance the jacket look, rounded collar with scalloped overcast edge, eyelet cutwork, pearl buttons.

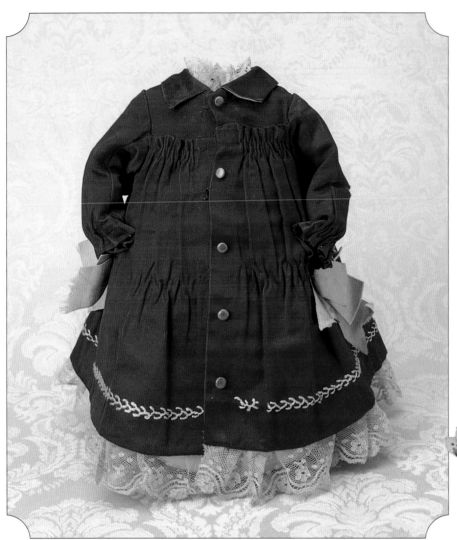

194. MAROON SILK BEBE FROCK
3" shoulder width. 9 1/2" overall length. One-piece costume with fitted yoke, shaped collar, gathered bodice with further gathers at hips, set-in sleeves with gathered cuffs, cotton sateen lining, hook and eye closure, lace lining at collar, lace edged hem, brass buttons, feather-stitch in aqua wool thread and aqua silk bows.

195. PALE GREEN VELVET BONNET
8" x 6". 4" inside head width. Plush green velvet bonnet has gathered full back, 2" gathered brim to cloister the face, green silk taffeta ribbons, bow and ties, border of ivory tatting.

196. IVORY SILK QUILTED BONNET
7" circular shape. 5" inside head width.
Designed to perch aside the head, the bonnet is constructed of quilted ivory silk, has border of silk box pleats, elaborate cluster of silk ribbons at crest, and interior fine lace border with silk loops, ivory silk ribbon and streamers.

197. BONE FAN WITH ROUNDED TIPS
3" L. blades. 13-blade fan folds/opens, has rounded tips, cutwork designs to capture breezes, interwoven silk ribbons.

198. BONE FAN WITH SILK RIBBONS
3 1/2" L. blades. 9-blade fan folds/opens, has cutwork and impressed designs, interwoven lavender and green silk ribbons.

199. TWO SMALL BEBE STAYS WITH MAKER'S SIGNATURES
8 3/4" and 9 1/4" waist sizes. Each of coutil, one with Art Nouveau leaf pattern with baby blue binding and straps, maker's stamp indicating its production as a model of child-sized stay, "Pour avoir un corset/Solide - Elegant - Bonne forme - demandez the marque F.P."; and second with ribbed designs, floral pattern, rose binding and straps, maker's stamp blurred. Each with brass grommets and lacing.

200. BEBE JUMEAU ENSEMBLE IN AQUA SILK AND VELVET
5" shoulder width. 13" waist. 7" skirt length. Figured aqua silk jacket dress has pleated yoke, stand-up collar with aqua braid edging, jacket front with wide lapels and braid edging forming box-pleated back of dress and long side lappets, lace overlay bodice, box-pleated Juliet sleeves, turn-up lace trimmed cuffs, box pleated skirt front with embroidered lace overlay, modified bustle with cartridge pleating and coiled braid trim, lace back collar, aqua silk ribbon trim. And aqua plush velvet bonnet with buckram form and 4 1/2" wired brim lined with tightly pleated aqua silk, ivory silk inner lining with script letter "9". And wooden-handled silk satin parasol with mechlin lace trim. And matching muslin chemise and petticoat with pleated trim, Bavarian lace. The costume was presented by Emile Jumeau, circa 1885 on his signature bebes, probably size 9.

201. IVORY SILK SATIN GOWN WITH TRAIN
5" shoulder width. 11" waist. 11" skirt front. Ivory silk satin gown has wide box pleats into V-shape, rolled collar band, set-in long sleeves with box-pleated bretelles, fitted waist, gored flat front skirt with muslin pleated dust ruffle, 22" extended train from gathered back. The gown is lined in cotton sateen and has ivory grosgrain ribbon sash and bows.

202. IVORY SILK SATIN DOUBLE-DRAPED CAPE
5 1/2" shoulder width. 10 1/2" length. Stitch-shaped shoulders allows the flared double-layered cape to drape smoothly, has delicate fringing, gold soutache trim, silk lining.

203. IVORY LIMERICK LACE CAPE
7 1/2" shoulder width. 7" length. Elaborately constructed cape of 2" bands of lace with embroidered floral detail has rolled collar, wide gussets at shoulders lends a flared look to the shoulder drape, the upper lace tier creates the effect of bretelles.

204. WOVEN AND SILK BONNET WITH BIRD
7 1/2" x 6 1/2" outside dimensions. 5" inside head width. Firmly shaped bonnet designed to perch atop the head has rolled-up narrow brim, is covered with draped and pleated ivory silk with lace detail, has woven straw bands in intricate fashion, and a woven straw bird at the very peak. Muslin lining with center cut-out revealing original "Paris" paper label.

205. HEAVILY RE-EMBROIDERED LINEN LACE FROCK WITH AQUA TRIM

8" shoulder width. 18" overall length. Ivory linen-lace frock is exquisitely constructed and delicately re-embroidered, has rounded collar with stand-up edge, demi-sleeves over wide aqua grosgrain ribbon, blue cotton plastron hidden under cutwork and bordered by grosgrain ribbon, dropped waist, gathered skirt, 2 1/2" wide aqua grosgrain sash with elaborate bow.

206. AQUA BLUE VELVET PURSE

6" length. Firm-sided purse is richly covered in soft aqua-blue velvet plush, has velvet bail handles, beautifully detailed brass hardware, little ball feet, clasp. The bag opens to reveal blue silk tufted interior.

207. BLUE SILK PARASOL

12" L. A wooden-handled parasol with fancy embossed brass hand-grip and tip, has original aqua-blue silk-satin cover decorated with silk loops and lace.

208. SILK BEBE STAYS WITH BLUE SILK BOWS

12 3/4" waist. Ivory silk stays have V-shaped darts at back waist, self-straps, very rich lace and blue silk ribbon trim, pearl button for attachment to pantaloons, brass grommets and original lacing.

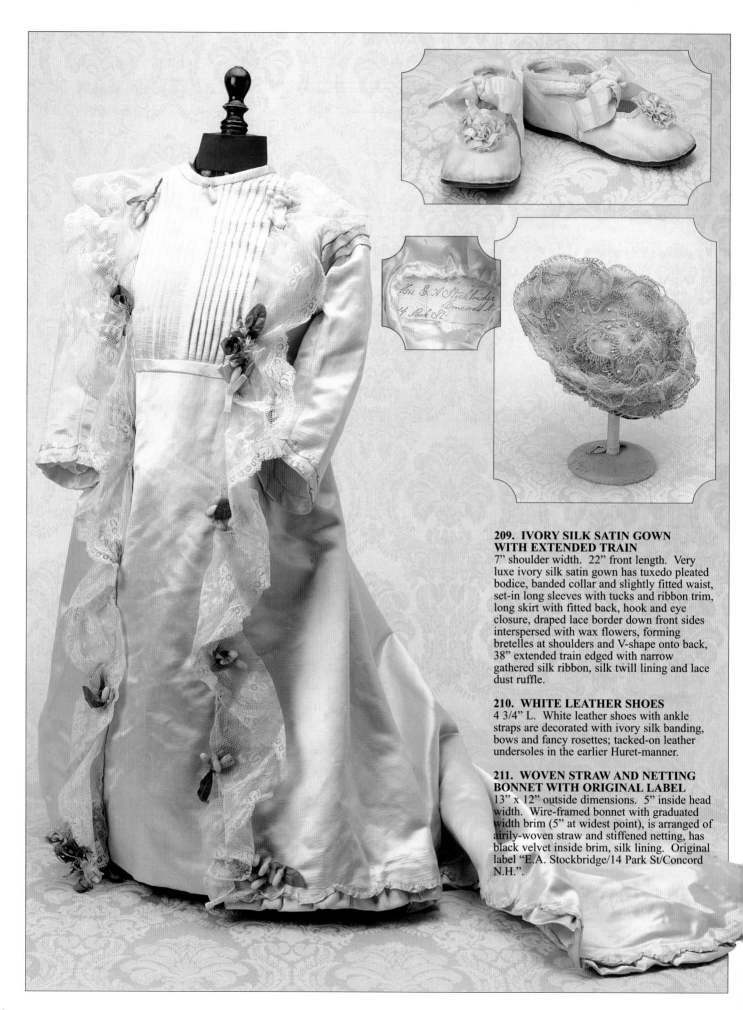

209. IVORY SILK SATIN GOWN WITH EXTENDED TRAIN
7" shoulder width. 22" front length. Very luxe ivory silk satin gown has tuxedo pleated bodice, banded collar and slightly fitted waist, set-in long sleeves with tucks and ribbon trim, long skirt with fitted back, hook and eye closure, draped lace border down front sides interspersed with wax flowers, forming bretelles at shoulders and V-shape onto back, 38" extended train edged with narrow gathered silk ribbon, silk twill lining and lace dust ruffle.

210. WHITE LEATHER SHOES
4 3/4" L. White leather shoes with ankle straps are decorated with ivory silk banding, bows and fancy rosettes; tacked-on leather undersoles in the earlier Huret-manner.

211. WOVEN STRAW AND NETTING BONNET WITH ORIGINAL LABEL
13" x 12" outside dimensions. 5" inside head width. Wire-framed bonnet with graduated width brim (5" at widest point), is arranged of airily-woven straw and stiffened netting, has black velvet inside brim, silk lining. Original label "E.A. Stockbridge/14 Park St/Concord N.H.".

212. FRENCH SILK ENSEMBLE BY EMILE JUMEAU

For size 10 bebe. 4 1/2" shoulder width. 12 1/2" waist. 8 1/4" skirt length. The ensemble comprises figured ivory silk frock with rich floral woven pattern having modified jacket front which hooks across the yoke, has lace-covered revealed bodice, box-pleated skirt with full back bustle decorated with back satin lined sash, V-shaped back bodice, bretelles over full-length set-in sleeves, full gauze and muslin lining. The frock is accented with cranberry-red silk satin bretelles, rolled collar, peplum, skirt edging and reticule, with additional red cording and Chantilly lace. And woven straw bonnet with elaborate wired red georgette brim, red satin streamers, red silk poppies and miniature flowers and leaves. And matching red silk shoes with overcast edging, maroon silk rosettes, red buttons, tan leather undersoles signed "10/Bebe Jumeau/Med d'Or 1878/Paris Depose" in gold letters, red knit stockings, muslin chemise with maroon silk ribbons, pantaloons.

213. WIRED GEORGETTE BONNET WITH SILK RIBBONS
15" x 11" outside dimensions. 5" inside head width. Buckram stiffened bonnet with graduated width (widest point 5") wired brim is covered with cream georgette, has very wide ivory silk ribbons and ties.

214. STRAW BONNET WITH WIRED BRIM
12" outside circumference. 5" inside head width. Fancily-woven straw cone-shaped bonnet has 2 1/2" ruffled cotton brim with wire-frame, ivory silk ribbon crest, muslin lining.

215. IVORY SILK ORGANZA BONNET WITH MILLINER'S LABEL
9" x 9" outside dimensions. 3" inside head width. Buckram-shaped bonnet is covered with sheer silk organza, decorated with ivory silk patterned ribbons and streamers, 3" organza-covered brim, ivory silk ruched border, silk lining with original label "Marie Vanderlinden/Bruxelles".

216. IVORY PLUSH BONNET WITH MILLINER'S LABEL
7" x 6" outside dimensions. 5" inside head width. Stiffened muslin form is covered with (worn) ivory plush, rolled self-edge, inner silk lining and lace face ruffle, ivory silk bow trim and ties. Original milliner's label (frail).

217. WHITE FUR FELT PEAKED BONNET
5" x 4 1/2" outside dimensions. 2" inside head width. Buckram-stiffened high-peaked bonnet is covered with lavish white fur felt and decorated with fancy white boa feather, ivory silk bows. The interior brim has pleated ivory silk lining, sheer silk interior lining.

218. WHITE WOOL FELT BONNET
5" x 5" outside dimensions. 2 1/2" inside head width. Buckram stiffened bonnet of white pressed wool felt has rounded top, draped ivory silk band with long white boa feathers, silk edging and pleated silk liner of inside brim, gauze head liner.

219. BLACK LEATHER SHOES SIGNED E.J.
3". Black kid leather shoes have brown edging, leather straps with gold bead closures, brown silk rosette decoration, tan leather soles signed E.J./Depose/8.

220. BLACK LEATHER SHOES, SIZE 1, FOR BRU
1 1/2". Black leather shoes with overcast brown edging, black button and elastic closures, black silk rosettes, leather soles signed B (in script) and 1. (one sole missing).

221. TAN LEATHER SHOES WITH MAROON BOWS
2". Tan leather shoes with leather straps captured by brown silk ribbons have maroon silk decorative bows held by silver buckles.

222. WHITE FUR FOX-TAIL STOLE IN ORIGINAL BOX
About 15". Thick white double-sided fur stole with black-tipped fox tail is decorated with white chiffon rosettes and silk buttons. Contained in original box with blue paper and doily edge lining, glass top with gold edging.

223. GILT FAUX WATCH AND WATCH PIN
1". Faux watch has Roman numeral glass-topped face, fancy metal case with gold finish, linked chain, and two-color watch pin in the shape of bird in flight.

224. GILT FAUX WATCH
3/4". Faux watch of similar design to #223 has linked chain.

225. BONE FRETWORK FAN
2 1/2" L. 15-blade bone fan with cutwork design, ribbon insertion.

226. BONE BALL AND CUP DOLL-SIZED TOY
3 1/2" cup. Artfully carved bone handle has "cup" top, green twill rope to which is strung a bone-carved ball. The object is to catch the ball in the cup. The popular child's toy was made in miniature size as doll accessory and is rarely found.

227. LAVENDER AND IVORY SILK STRIPED GOWN
5" shoulder width. 9" waist. 10" skirt length. The one-piece gown has very full gathers at shoulders held in place by corded tabs at front and back, square-cut neckline with reversed pattern of stripes, self-piping, very full long sleeves with 1" cuffs having 3 pearl buttons, fitted waist with very narrow pleats, self belt, 1" skirt fringe.

228. RED VELVET JACKET AND TAM
4 1/2" shoulder width. 9 3/4" length. Cranberry maroon jacket with set-in sleeves, maroon silk lining, maroon cord neck trim and ties, hook and eye closure. With matching tam, self-brim with velvet bow.

229. FRENCH BROWN LEATHER TRAVELING BAG
7" x 3 1/2". Brown leather traveling bag is ornamented with gold tooled stripes, has leather straps and bail handle, maroon fringe trim; unfolds to reveal interior with maroon silk moire lining, an assortment of toiletry articles including mirror and silver tipped hair comb. Stamped gold maker's mark (indecipherable).

230. WHITE LEATHER WRIST GLOVES
2 1/2". Soft white kid leather wrist gloves have cast-bound edging, defined thumbs, real buttonholes for white pearl buttons.

**231. GREY FUR MUFF IN ORIGINAL
AU BON MARCHE BOX**
3" L. Shaded grey/white plush fur muff is lined with red silk, has red silk ribbon neck ties. Contained in original blue paper box with rich gold stencilled label from Au Bon Marche, Paris.

232. BLUE VELVET CAPE AND BONNET
5 1/2" shoulder width. 7" length. Double-draped blue velvet cape has gold cord edging, hook and eye closure at neck, green silk lining, gathered stand-up collar at back of neck. And blue velvet bonnet trimmed with lighter blue grosgrain and silk streamers, bows and edging, lining.

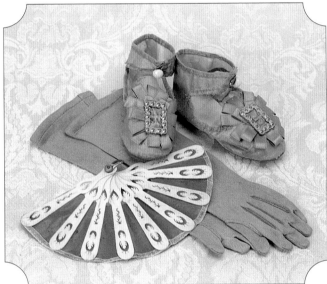

233. BLUE AND IVORY STRIPED SILK TWO-PIECE COSTUME
4" shoulder width. 12" waist. 7 3/4" skirt length. Of ice-blue silk and ivory
narrow pinstripes, comprising jacket with pleated lace plastron flanked by double row of pearl buttons,
dart-shaped back with long tails with additional pearl button trim, rolled collar band with lace collar
trim, set-in sleeves with lace and silk ribbon trim, cotton sateen lining; and skirt with flat front, box-
pleated back, 2" border of duchesse lace, and net lining.

234. TEAL VELVET PURSE WITH SILVER TRIM AND GOLD FOBS
6 1/2" x 5 1/2". Firm-sided bombe-shaped purse is covered with rich teal-blue velvet, has velvet bail
hand with knotted top and gold bands, hinges open to reveal rich tufted teal silk interior with some
'objets necessaire'. The exterior is decorated with superb silver decorative plates, embossed floral
design, and, cascading from the handle, two gold watch fobs.

235. BLUE SILK PARTY SHOES WITH SILVER BUCKLES
3 1/2" L. Soft-sided blue silk shoes are banded with narrow blue silk ribbons, have pearl button and
loop closures, silk looped rosette decoration with silver embossed buckles, leather soles in the Huret
manner with unusual embossed markings.

236. GREY SILK ELBOW GLOVES
6 1/2" L. Grey silk elbow-length gloves are seamed and hemmed, have set-in thumbs with finished
seams, decorative piping.

237. BONE FRETWORK FAN WITH BLUE LINING
2 1/2" L. 9-blade bone fan has unusual fretwork design which extends to lower blades, is lined with
blue silk taffeta twill, has gilt handle.

238. GREY SILK PLAID FROCK
3" shoulder width. 8" waist. 9 3/4" overall length. Of diminutive grey plaid, the one-piece frock has
fitted waist, hip sash with diamond-shaped petals over the box-pleated skirt, brown cotton sateen lining,
ice-blue silk trim, silver buttons.

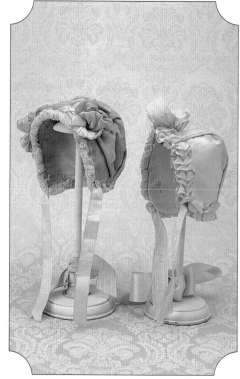

239. ROSE SILK SATIN BLOUSE
6" shoulder width. 19" waist. Fine quality rose silk satin blouse has pleated bodice overlaid with 1" rose silk banners decorated with ivory embroidery, puffed short sleeves, cotton muslin lining with back string ties, lavish 2" width ivory lace trim on bodice, neckline, sleeves, and three rose silk taffeta ribbon bows.

240. ROSE VELVET WIRED BONNET
5" x 4" outside dimension. 4" inside head width. Wire-framed bonnet with gathered and pleated velvet cover has rose cotton muslin lining, rolled lace edging, rose silk bows and streamers.

241. ROSE SILK SATIN BONNET
3 1/2" x 5". Rose silk satin cap has seamed fit with cord trim, cotton muslin lining, decorated around the face with pleated and ruffled pink Swiss embroidery ribbons and bows, pencil inscribed "10" on interior.

242. PINK STRIPED SILK STOCKINGS
5" foot length. 11" leg length. Horizontally striped rose and ivory silk stockings have sewn-in toes and heels.

243. KNIT WOOL MITTS
2 1/2" L. Tiny knit pattern is evident on the white wool gloves with drawstring wrists, rose edging.

244. BLACK FLOWERED COUTIL BEBE STAY
9" waist. Black coutil is patterned with delicate pink flowers and trailing vines, has pink silk ruched edging, tapered straps of same fabric, lace trim, four bone inserts, brass lacing grommets.

245. ROSE SILK SATIN BEBE STAYS, SIZE 12, FOR BEBE JUMEAU
15" waist. Rose silk satin stays are lined with white cotton, have corded stitching for strength, lace edging, straps, three pearl buttons for attachment to pantaloons, brass lacing grommets, signed "12".

246. WHITE COTTON SATEEN BEBE STAY, SIZE 1O, FOR BEBE JUMEAU
12" waist. Heavy white cotton sateen stay has cording for decoration and strength, brass lacing grommets, pearl buttons for attachment to pantaloons, shoulder straps, rose ribbon and lace trim. Marked "10".

248. WHITE LEATHER SHOES SIGNED C.C.
2 1/2" L. White leather shoes have grosgrain silk edging, leather straps with gold bead closures, silk and lace rosettes, leather soles signed C.C./4.

249. ROSE SATIN SILK PARTY GOWN WITH MATCHING BONNET
4 1/2" shoulder width. 11" waist. 15" overall length. Rose satin silk gown with V-shaped waist, square neckline, double-seamed long sleeves, hook and eye closure; with skirt having slightly extended back, cording trim. The gauze-lined skirt is overlaid with re-embroidered and pearl-encrusted lace, appliqued beading and beaded sash. With matching gauze-lined cap trimmed with lace, beads, and pearls.

250. BONE FRETWORK FAN
2" L. 14-blade cut-work fan has inset lavender silk ribbon.

251. BONE CUTWORK FAN WITH HAND-PAINTED SILK
2 1/2" L. 10-blade cut-work fan has ivory silk cover with hand-painted roses, gold edging.

252. WHITE LEATHER GLOVES
3" L. White leather gloves have brown overcast edging and decoration.

Costumes, Bonnets, Shoes And Accessories, 1875-1890

80

Costumes, Bonnets, Shoes And Accessories, 1875-1890

253. STRAW BONNET WITH MAROON VELVET AND SATEEN
6 1/2" x 6 1/2" outside dimensions. 2 1/2" inside head width. Formed from very narrow bands of straw woven in intricate manner with multi-dimensional effect, the inside brim lined with maroon velvet, the outside decorated with maroon cotton sateen ribbons and silk flowers. Ivory cotton sateen lining.

254. INTERWOVEN STRAW BONNET WITH PLEATED BRIM
6" x 5" outside dimensions. 3 1/2" inside head width. Rounded bonnet which frames the face and ties under the chin with silk chiffon ties is formed by an unusual cross-weaving of wide and thread-like straw. The brim is a double row of box pleats of the same unusual woven combination, trimmed with tiny white flowers and silk ribbons.

255. BRAIDED STRAW BONNET WITH ROSE GROSGRAIN RIBBON
7" x 7" outside dimensions. 3" inside head width. The bonnet, designed to sit atop the head, is created from narrow braided straw bands enhanced with little straw curls, decorated with rose silk grosgrain bow.

256. STRAW BONNET WITH IVORY SILK RIBBONS
6" x 6" outside dimensions. 2 1/2" inside head width. Designed to sit atop the head, the flat-topped bonnet has wide brim, is criss-crossed with ivory silk bands which extend across the brim to form tie-bands; the edge is decorated with narrow braid and tiny gold medallions.

257. BLACK STRAW DUCKBILL BONNET
5" x 6" outside dimensions. 2 1/2" inside head width. Woven straw bonnet with duckbill brim is tinted black with rich glazed effect, the inside duckbill brim lined with pleated black silk twill and decorated with black beads; the outside decorated with black feathers and black grosgrain ribbon.

258. STRAW BONNET WITH MAROON SILK TRIM
5" x 6" outside dimensions. 3" inside head width. Narrow bands of woven straw are assembled in an intricate manner with upturned brim at the front, red straw outer band, five maroon silk ribbon loops atop, ivory silk ribbon decoration on front brim.

259. BRAIDED STRAW DUCKBILL BONNET WITH LINEN LACE LINING
7" x 5 1/2" outside dimensions. 1 1/2" inside head width. Narrow bands of braided straw in natural color form a bonnet with flatter, rounded cap, graduated width brim with 3" duckbill brim at top, decorated with figured ivory silk bows and ribbons. The inside brim is lined with ivory linen lace and is visible when hat is worn.

260. WOVEN STRAW BONNET WITH CURLED STRAW BRIM
6" x 5" outside dimensions. 2" inside head width. Designed to perch atop the head, the woven straw bonnet has vertical straw rays on brim, one side of brim upturned for jaunty effect, rolled edge. The brim is banded by a cluster of narrow straw curls. Dyed red straw is interwoven to outer edge and forms a bow, appearing to be a silk ribbon.

261. PALE GREEN WOVEN STRAW BONNET WITH SILK CHIFFON
8" x 7" outside dimension. 2 1/2" inside head width. Pale green tinted straw bonnet has flat top, graduated width brim that is very high, "4", on top, decorated inside and outside with richly draped sheer silk chiffon and tiny straw curls.

262. WOVEN BONNET WITH GEORGETTE TRIM
9" x 10" outside dimensions. 4" inside head width. Bands of elaborately woven very fine straw has medallion center, 4" wide brim, layered georgette, silk lining. The seemingly large bonnet is actually sized for very small head.

263. TULLE BONNET WITH SILK RIBBON TRIM
8" x 7" outside dimensions. 5" inside head width. Ivory tulle bonnet with pleats has wired edge, bordered small ruffle with thick cluster of box pleats and gathers at the crest is decorated with clusters of very narrow silk ribbons, silk ribbon streamers.

264. LACE BONNET WITH SILK RIBBONS
6" x 5" outside dimensions. 4" inside head width. Constructed of narrow bands of lace and Swiss embroidery with medallion center back, lace ruffled trim, banded by thick lace ruffles, tulle crown interwoven with narrow ivory silk lace ribbons, stiffening around the face, ivory silk ribbons.

265. LACE PARTY FROCK AND BONNET WITH MILLINER'S LABEL
6" shoulder width. 15" waist. 11" skirt length. Party frock constructed of horizontal bands of lace and alternate bands of silk ribbon-threaded lace, the frock has V-shaped yoke with ribbon trim, 2" Bertha lace collar, demi-sleeves, rose silk underslip, button and loop closure. And woven straw bonnet with graduated width brim trimmed on the underside with very fine lace, flowers and rose silk ribbons; the topside is trimmed with more lace, tiny white flowers and four rose silk rosettes. Silk lining and original milliner's label "Mrs E.C. Tompkins/Fine millinery/348 Main St/Cor. Academy/Poughkeepsie, N.Y."

266. COUTIL CORSET WITH BOSOM AND HIP GUSSETS
10" waist. 5 1/2" L. Ivory coutil corset is elaborately constructed with gussets and shaping at bosom and hips, has inset boning, ivory embroidery, brass grommets and lacing; crochet-lace and ivory silk ribbon decorate the upper edge.

267. WOOL FELT BONNET
5" x 4 1/2" outside dimensions. 2 1/2" inside head width. Of ivory wool felt, the firm-sided bonnet is designed to sit atop the head, has flat top, narrow brim, patterned ivory silk draped band and bow, feather trim, the inside brim is lined with same silk fabric, sheer ivory silk lining.

268. HORSEHAIR BONNET WITH TINY ROSES, MILLINER'S LABEL
5 1/2" x 6" outside dimensions. 3" inside head width. Designed to perch atop the head, the bonnet is constructed of stiffened horsehair sewn in narrow band, decorated with overlay stiffened lace trimmed with straw "jewels", silk ruched band, coronet of tiny roses and rose buds, pale rose silk streamers. Cotton sateen lining with gold stamped label "Registered Palermo", and green paper label for Gregory Cubitt.

269. BLACK LEATHER SHOES SIGNED C.M.
2" L. Of soft black kid leather with white stitching, ankle strap with double silver buttons, brown silk rosettes, tan soles marked "C.M."

269A. BLACK LEATHER SHOES SIGNED E.J.
3" L. Soft black kid leather shoes have brown overcast edging, ankle straps with black button closure, brown silk rosettes, tan soles with incised detail around edges, marked E.J. (elaborately intertwined) and 10 (one sole missing).

269C. BLACK LEATHER SHOES SIGNED C.M.
2 1/2" L. Soft black kid leather shoes have (worn) brown silk edging, brown silk rosettes, ankle straps with double black button, tan soles marked "C.M." and 2.

270. BLACK LEATHER SHOES SIGNED C.M.
2 1/2" L. Soft black leather shoes with iridescent glister, white stitched edging, brown silk ribbon ties, brown silk rosettes, tan undersoles marked "C.M." and 3.

271. BLACK LEATHER SHOES WITH GREYHOUND SYMBOL
3" L. Soft black leather shoes with white stitching, ankle straps with buckles and buttons, red inner soles, brown silk rosettes, tan soles with incised symbol of resting greyhound.

272. WHITE LEATHER SHOES SIGNED "AU NAIN BLEU"
1 1/2" L. Soft white kid leather shoes with very wide ankle straps, white overcast stitching, cord ties, white pompoms, light tan soles signed "Au Nain Bleu" and 3. The prestige Parisian boutique commissioned special costumes for their dolls.

273. WHITE LEATHER SHOES SIGNED "BEBE JUMEAU"
3" L. Soft white kid leather with white overcast edging, ivory silk ties on ankle straps, ivory silk bows, tan undersoles signed "Bebe Jumeau Depose" and 9.

274. BLACK LEATHER SHOES SIGNED "BEBE NADAUD"
2" L. Black leather shoes with iridescent finish, brown overcast edging, loop and black button closure, brown silk rosettes, tan undersoles signed "Bebe Nadaud/34 rue de 4 Septembre/Paris/Depose" and 4. Bebes Jumeau were commissioned by the Nadaud boutique and wore their custom clothes.

275. TAN LEATHER FRENCH-LIKE GERMAN SHOES
1 3/4" L. Stiff tan leather shoes with overcast edging, brown silk button closures, brown silk rosettes, light-yellow soles signed with elaborately scrolled (indecipherable) initials and "Made in Germany".

276. BLACK LEATHER SHOES FOR BEBE BRU
1 1/2" L. Soft black kid leather shoes with brown overcast edging, brass button closures at ankle straps, brown silk ribbons, ivory undersoles signed "B" in scroll and 2.

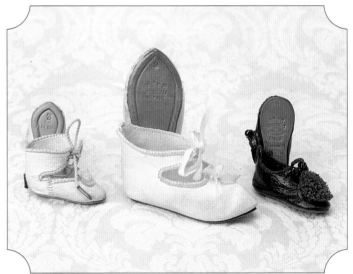

277. BLACK LEATHER SHOES
2" L. Soft black kid leather shoes with iridescent finish, light-tan overcast edging, ankle straps with loop closures, delicate silk floral decorations, signed 3.

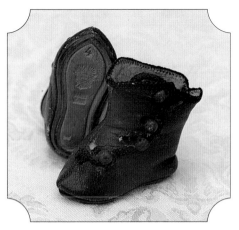  

278. BLACK LEATHER BOOTS SIGNED PARIS BEBE
1 3/4". Soft black kid leather ankle boots with front flaps, four button closure, tan undersoles signed Paris Bebe Paris Depose and 4.

279. BLACK LEATHER BOOTS SIGNED L.P.
2 1/2" L. Soft black kid leather boots have brown overcast stitching, three lacing grommets, brown cord laces, brown silk rosettes, tan undersoles signed L.P. and 8.

280. BROWN LEATHER HEELED BOOTS
2 3/4" L. Soft brown kid leather boots with narrow brown silk banding, six gold lacing buttons, black heels, tan undersoles.

281. BLACK LEATHER BOOTS SIGNED L.D.
3" L. Soft black kid leather boots with brown overcast edging have 3 pairs of lacing grommets, original brown laces, silk rosettes, signed L.D. and 9.

282. BLACK LEATHER SHOES SIGNED "A LA PROVIDENCE"
4" L. Soft black kid leather shoes have very wide double-laced ankle straps, brown overcast stitching, brown laces, brown silk rosettes, dark brown soles signed with figure of doll in chemise and "A La Providence/74 rue de Rivoli" and 11.

283. TWELVE PAIR OF JUMEAU SOCKS
Of various sizes, the openwork knit cotton socks are in various colors including black, cranberry, cream, blue, tan and rose.

284. MAUVE VELVET PURSE
6" L. Arch-shaped firm-sided purse is covered with soft silk velvet plush, has elaborate silver bead frame and fancy clasp, monogram crest on front, bail handle, tiny silver ball feet, hinges open to reveal silk lined interior with mirror.

285. SILK BROCADE FROCK
7" shoulder width. 15" waist. 13" skirt length. Of very fine silk brocade with tiny floral pattern, the changeable color varies from mauve to green, with fitted bodice, rolled collar, inset pleated sleeves, 1 1/2" cuffs, ivory silk ruched yoke, double row of ruching below the waist, fully lined, hook and eye closure.

286. GREEN VELVET BONNET AND SILK MUFF AND COLLAR WITH BOA FEATHER TRIM
6" L. muff. Padded green silk muff has black velvet criss-crossed ribbon trim, boa feather edges, cluster of fabric bluet floral trim, silk ivory bows. With matching boa-trimmed collar. And green velvet bonnet with wired brim, ivory tatted trim, ivory silk ruffled ribbon trim and large bows, silk liner, original label "Magasin du Louvre/Paris".

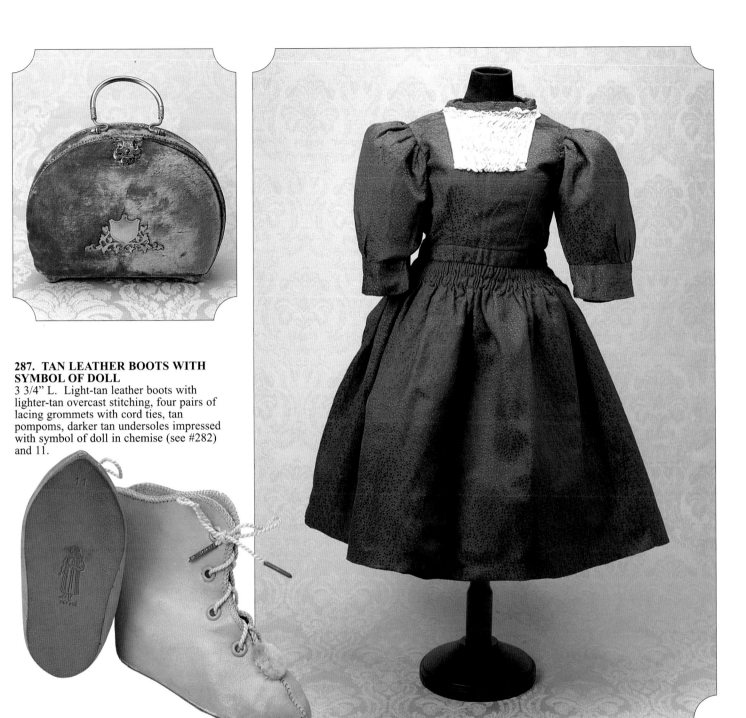

287. TAN LEATHER BOOTS WITH SYMBOL OF DOLL
3 3/4" L. Light-tan leather boots with lighter-tan overcast stitching, four pairs of lacing grommets with cord ties, tan pompoms, darker tan undersoles impressed with symbol of doll in chemise (see #282) and 11.

CHAPTER FOUR
Undergarments, 1880-1915

288. WHITE LAWN CHILD'S DAY DRESS
6" shoulder width. 16" drawstring waist. 12" skirt length.
Fine white cotton lawn dress with square-cut drawstring
neckline framed by 1" piped and embroidered band,
scalloped edging, tucks and scalloped trim on demi-
sleeves, bodice and skirt gathered by draw-string waist.

289. FOUR-PIECE BEBE UNDERGARMENTS
7" shoulder width. 12" waist. Comprising white cotton
full slip with double ruffle at back, drop waist, button
closure; white wool slip thickly knitted for warmth; white
cotton pantaloons with drawstring lace edging on legs; and
white cotton chemise with floral embroidery and "Bebe".

290. WHITE MUSLIN NIGHTSHIRT
6" shoulder width. 17" overall length. Loosely-fitted
long nightshirt has tucked bodice, cutwork-edged placket
and stand-up collar, set-in sleeves with cutwork ruffles on
cuffs, monogrammed SC.

**291. WHITE MUSLIN NIGHTSHIRT WITH
EMBROIDERED TRIM**
6" shoulder width. 16" length. Muslin nightshirt has
triple tucks at either side of placket opening, red and blue
Schiffli embroidery on stand-up collar, ruffled placket and
ruffled cuffs.

**292. WHITE MUSLIN NIGHTSHIRT
WITH CROSS-BAR LACE**
7" shoulder width. 20" overall length. White muslin
nightshirt with narrow tucks down the entire front, full-
length placket with scalloped and cross-bar lace, enhanced
with embroidery, cutwork and embroidered cuffs and
collar.

293. WHITE COTTON SMOCK
7" shoulder width. 22" length. White cotton nightshirt
with open back, square-cut neck with button back, set-in
full sleeve with buttoned cuffs, two
pockets, scalloped overcast edging at
neck, hem, pockets and cuffs.

**294. PAIR, MUSLIN
NIGHTSHIRTS**
Each 6" shoulder width. 18" overall
length. Matched pair of nightgowns
have fitted bodice, gathered full front,
set-in full sleeves with lace trimmed
cuffs, rounded Peter Pan collars with
lace edging, button closures.

288

289

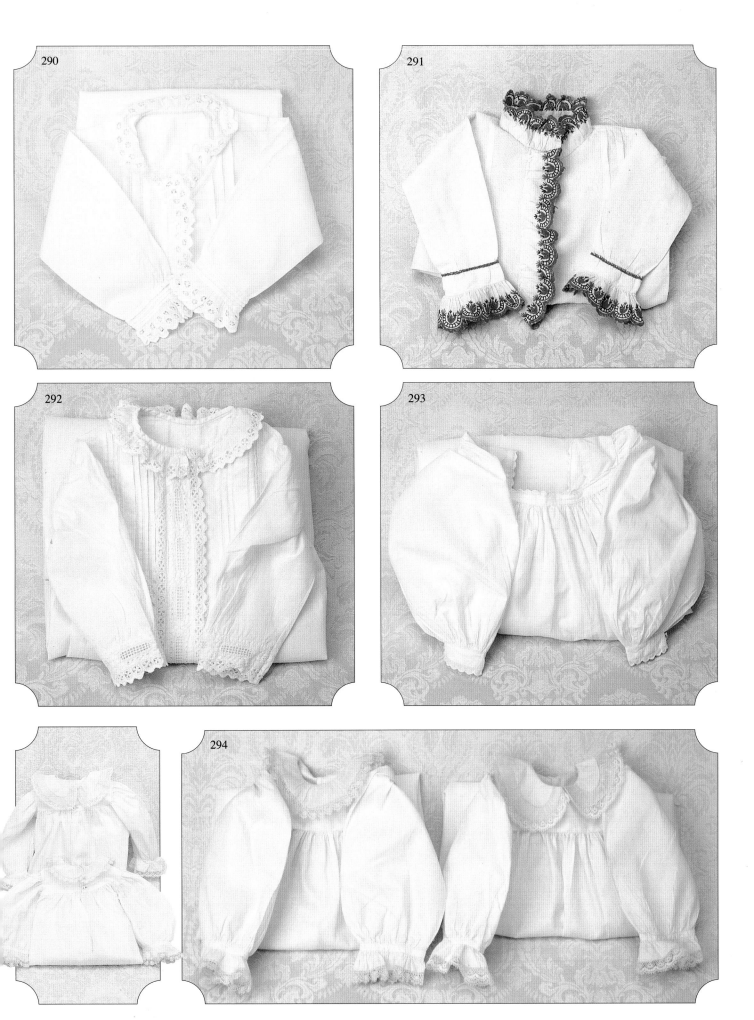

295. FOUR-PIECE BEBE UNDERGARMENTS
4 1/2" shoulder width. 10" waist. 11" overall length. Comprising white linen chemise dress with 1" band drawstring waist, scalloped overcast edging at square bodice, demi-sleeves, pleated skirt; red flannel chemise with muslin lined quilted bodice; coutil bebe stays with lacing grommets; and white jacket with red embroidered trim at neckline, hem and cuffs of set-in sleeves.

296. FIVE-PIECE COTTON UNDERGARMENTS
6" waist. 7" overall length. Muslin undergarments comprise straight-cut chemise with red stitching at bodice, monogrammed "C"; full slip with gathered skirt and matching pantaloons with cutwork and red embroidered detail; petticoat with cutwork and red tulip embroidery, lace hem edging; handkerchief.

297. FOUR-PIECE BEBE UNDERGARMENTS
About 6" shoulder width. 10" waist. Comprising white muslin waist-length chemise with lace edging and set-in sleeves; beige flannel full-length slip with pleated bodice, scalloped hem with overcast stitches, button straps; pique bebe stays with lacing grommets; print muslin apron with Schiffli embroidery.

298. FOUR COTTON PETTICOATS
7" - 16" waist. Of various sizes, various fabrics from fine cottons to muslin, various trims including cutwork, lace, tucks, and embroidery, the petticoats illustrate the wide possibilities in decoration presented on early undergarments.

299. THREE UNDERGARMENTS
4 1/2" - 5 1/2" shoulder width. Of various cottons, the lot includes chemisette with overcast scalloped edging, fitted waist, button back; and two simple chemises, one with overcast scalloped edging, one with handkerchief edge.

300. FOUR-PIECE BEBE UNDERGARMENTS FOR SIZE 12 BEBE JUMEAU
14" waist. 13" overall slip length. Of white cotton, comprising matched slip and pantaloons with scalloped ruffled cutwork edging, tucks, button-closure, dart fitting on slip bodice; peach-colored coutil bebe stays with lace edging, lacing grommets, labelled "12", and 5 1/2" square handkerchief with tucks and lace edging.

301. FOUR-PIECE BEBE UNDERGARMENTS FOR SIZE 10 BEBE JUMEAU
12" waist. 13" overall slip length. Of white cotton, comprising pleated pantaloons with double button closures, scalloped cutwork trim; full-length pique slip with dart-fitted bodice, cutwork cotton trim; drawstring waist petticoat with lace edging; and white cotton sateen bebe stays with lacing grommets.

302. THREE-PIECE BEBE UNDERGARMENTS
14" waist. 12" skirt length. Comprising white cotton
pantaloons and petticoat with matching 1 1/2" ruffled
cutwork edging on hem, drawstring waist on petticoat;
with white cotton bebe stays, with lacing grommets.

303. FOUR-PIECE BEBE UNDERGARMENTS
11 1/2" waist. 7" skirt length. Comprising muslin
petticoat with drawstring waist and double lace-trimmed
skirt; gathered cotton petticoat with button waist, soutache
and cotton trim; full slip with 1 1/2" lace edging; and
coutil stays with straps and pearl button pantaloon-
attachments.

304. FIVE BEBE STAYS
12" - 22" waist. Four with lacing grommets at back (fifth
with wrap-around self-fabric straps which button in front),
of various materials including patterned silk, brocade silk,
embroidered coutil, elastic, with lace, crocheted lace and
braided trim.

305. FOUR-PIECE BEBE UNDERGARMENTS
12" waist. 10" overall slip length. Of fine muslin, comprising short slip and short panties with Valenciennes lace trim, and coutil bebe stays with brocade design, laced back, crochet lace straps and trim, buttons for attachment to panties which have corresponding button hole.

306. COTTON SATEEN CHEMISETTE
13" fitted waist. Of fine cotton sateen with full-cut bodice, fitted waist with button closure, intricate rows of tucks, Swiss embroidery with interwoven rose silk ribbons, cutwork ruffled edging at neckline and sleeves.

307. FOUR-PIECE BATISTE COTTON ENSEMBLE
9" waist. 8" skirt length. Of fine white cotton batiste, the set comprises two petticoats, pantaloons and chemisette with drawstring top and button waist, each trimmed in matching broderie Anglaise lace.

308. THREE-PIECE COTTON ORGANDY ENSEMBLE
6" waist. 9" skirt length. Of sheer cotton organdy, the set comprises petticoat and pantaloons with button waist, long chemise. Each is trimmed with multi-rows of tucks (the chemise with unique all-around vertical tucks), blue silk ribbon inserts, lace edging.

309. THREE-IN-ONE UNDERGARMENT
7" waist. 10" overall. One-piece muslin undergarment comprises three functions: chemise, pants, and slip, and is uniquely constructed, has lace edging, aqua silk ribbon inserts, button waist.

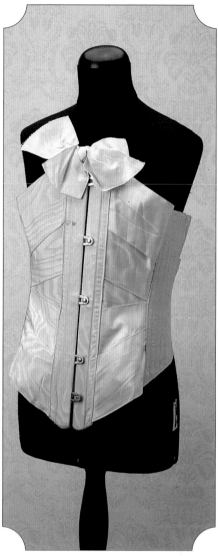

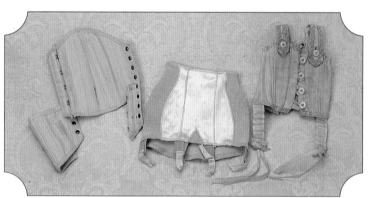

310. LADY'S UNDERGARMENT ENSEMBLE
10" waist. 11" skirt. Three-piece set comprises fitted corset with brocade flowers, laced back; corset cover with tucked yoke, pearl button, lace trim; and full-length slip with six rows of banding and lace at hemline, blue silk ribbon inserts, button back.

311. LADY'S IVORY SILK MOIRE CORSET WITH PATENT DATE
18" waist. Ivory silk moire corset has boning at sides and back,
metal hooks at front, lacing at back, ribbon and bow trim. The hooks are marked "Patented/Feb. 9, 1897".

312. THREE CORSETS
7" - 8" waist. Three unusual variations of corsets include: ivory silk stays with lace back, button front, straps, and attached garters; rose coutil corset with boning, unusual low-cut back, marked "Charls/US Trademark"; and elastic girdle with rose silk satin front panel, garter attachments.

313. FOUR BEBE STAYS
6" - 12" waists. Coutil and silk bebe stays represent wide variety of styles, including blue patterned silk twill with laced back, three examples with all-around boning, lacing, and slight waist shaping.

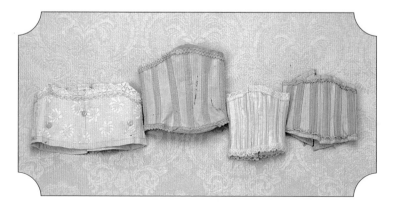

CHAPTER FIVE

Baby Costumes And Accessories, 1880-1910

314. FIVE-PIECE WHITE PIQUE BABY ENSEMBLE
7" shoulder width. 14" waist. 26" overall length. White pique ensemble comprises baby gown with snugly-fit, V-shaped, scalloped bodice, eyelet edged neck, long set-in sleeves with rolled up cuffs, four fabric buttons, box-pleated skirt; coat with very full gathers, 11" L. capelet collar with braid and cutwork trim; jacket with ruffled collar and turn-up scalloped cuffs; petticoat with button straps; and diaper with pearl buttons.

315. BATISTE BABY GOWN AND SLIP
7" shoulder width. 40" overall length. Delicate white batiste baby gown has embroidered floral-pattern yoke, vertical bands of inset lace, lace ruffle trim, gathered lower bodice, high waist with piping detail, long sleeves with 1" lace borders, gathered skirt, six button-closure back. And white cotton slip with drawstring neckline, scalloped edge short sleeves, gathered and drawstring waist.

316. LACE BABY BONNET
4" x 6" outside head dimension. 5" inside head width. Exquisite Broderie Anglaise lace bonnet with tiny details of workmanship have double row of Valenciennes lace ruffles, silk satin lining, patterned ivory silk bows and streamers.

317. PAIR, IVORY SILK BABY BIBS
9" overall length. 3" neck size. Matching pair of ivory silk baby bibs are lined and quilted in elaborate pattern, lace-edged at neck, scalloped lace around the exterior, pearl button closures.

318. WHITE COTTON BABY GOWN
7" shoulder width. 36" overall front length. White cotton baby gown has elaborate inset panels down the entire front length, comprising gathers, cutwork, edging, and ruffles. The trim is of progressively larger borders from top to bottom, and the length is slightly greater in the rear; three pearl button closure.

319. WHITE COTTON BABY GOWN AND HALF-SLIP
7" shoulder width. 42" overall length. Delicate white cotton baby gown has scooped rounded neckline trimmed with lace and draw-string ties, set-in gathered high waist, elaborate front panel which extends the entire front of skirt and composed of alternate bands of tucks, insert lace, ruffles, 3" band of lace at hemline. With matching half-slip having rows of tuckings at hemline.

Baby Costumes And Accessories, 1880-1910

320. WHITE BATISTE BABY GOWN

4" shoulder width. 24" overall length. Fine batiste cotton baby gown has rounded collar, very full short sleeves with wide ruffled Swiss embroidery and cutwork, graduated width of entire front with insert bands of lace and cutwork, long ruffled borders, 3" ruffled hem, muslin-lined bodice with fitted and buttoned back. And white pique baby cape with hand-hemmed edges and collar, cutwork trim.

321. TWO BABY BLANKETS

Comprising 30" square cream plush wool blanket with pinked scalloped edges, cutwork slits through which is drawn silk maroon ribbon, and embroidered word "Baby"; and 35" x 31" white wool flannel baby blanket with fold-over top, padded quilted lining, lace edging, 6" border of lace trim, and very dramatic ivory silk satin bow.

322. MUSLIN BLUE-FLOWERED CHEMISE FOR JUMEAU
4" shoulder width. 11 3/4" waist. 12" overall length. For size 8 or 9 Bebe Jumeau. White muslin is printed with tiny bluets, has accordion pleated bodice and hem ruffle with lace edging, blue threaded stitching, white lace at collar, full short sleeves, box pleated front from below the bodice clinched by separate matching belt, pleated dust ruffles at hemline, narrow blue silk ribbon trim. Red silk Bebe Jumeau banner at waist. The signature fabric and chemise was registered by Jumeau in 1892.

323. MUSLIN BLUE FLOWERED CHEMISE FOR JUMEAU
6 1/4" shoulder width. 18" waist. 17 1/2" overall length. For size 13 or 14 Bebe Jumeau. Of identical construction and fabric to #322 except larger and without red Bebe Jumeau banner.

324. BLUE-TRIMMED MUSLIN CHEMISE
3" shoulder width. 8" overall length. Stiffened muslin chemise has loose box pleats the entire length, stand-up collar, puffed sleeves, shadow lace over blue muslin trim at hem, cuffs, collar, ruffled yoke and separate belt.

325. MUSLIN RED FLOWERED CHEMISE FOR JUMEAU
5 1/4" shoulder width. 16" waist. 15" overall length. For size 11 or 12 Bebe Jumeau. Of identical construction and fabric to #322 except larger and having red flowers and ribbon.

326. WHITE GAUZE CHEMISE
5 3/4" shoulder width. 16" overall length. White gauze chemise has gathered yoke with Valenciennes lace trim, puffed shorts, Cluny lace at hem and sleeve edges, drawstring neck.

327. MUSLIN RED FLOWERED CHEMISE FOR JUMEAU'S BEBE PARLANT
4" shoulder width. 10 1/2" overall length. For size 7 or 8 Bebe Jumeau. Of identical construction and fabric to #322 except red flowers (washed and faded) and having two brass-edged grommets at side to allow the protrusion of Mama/Papa pull-strings.

CHAPTER SEVEN
Mariner Costumes, 1890-1910

328. STRIPED COTTON MUSLIN MIDDY COSTUME
5" shoulder width. 10" waist. The two-piece ensemble of heavy red and white pencil-striped muslin comprises hip-length middy jacket with breast pocket, set-in 3/4 sleeves with cuffs, white pique middy collar and separate dickey, Swiss embroidered detail on collar, separate white pique belt, belt loops; and matching short trousers with fly-front.

329. RED MUSLIN MARINER COSTUME
4" shoulder width. 8 1/2" waist. 9" skirt length. Two-piece ensemble of bright red muslin comprises hip-length jacket with gathered fitting at back, middy-trimmed front placket with button closure, white sailor collar with embroidered anchors, grosgrain cuffs, separate belt; and graduated width knife-pleated skirt with double row of grosgrain braid.

329A. HENRIETTA WOOL PLAID MARINER-STYLE FROCK
6" shoulder width. 15 1/2" overall length. Richly patterned woven Henrietta wool one-piece costume has deep V-shaped bodice with wide ivory silk faille collar trimmed with 11 rows of trapunto stitching, hoop and eye attached plastron and roll-up cuffs with trapunto stitch trim, full-length front and back box pleats, belt loops, moire ribbon belt with mother-of-pearl buckle, full cotton sateen lining.

330. WOOL GABARDINE MARINER COSTUME WITH ANCHORS
5 3/4" shoulder width. 16" waist. 8 1/2" skirt length. One-piece mariner frock with blouson top, hook and eye front hidden closure, middy collar, separate V-shaped dickey, set-in sleeves, knife-pleated skirt, richly banded middy braid trim and hand-embroidered anchors and rope; and matching cap with white pompom, blue silk streamers with embroidered anchors.

331. BOY'S BLUE LINEN MARINER SUIT
5 1/2" shoulder width. 13" pants waist. 9" pants length. Finely-woven navy blue linen ensemble comprises hip-length middy jacket with three-button front, narrow silk twill ribbon stripes, constructed pockets with twill piping, full muslin lining; and dart-shaped 3/4 length pants with button-fly-front, fully lined.

332. BLUE WOOL TWILL MARINER COSTUME
7" shoulder width. 16" waist. 8" skirt length. Three-piece ensemble comprising hip-length jacket with gathered hem, button front, blue cotton sailor-style collar and turn-up cuffs with middy braid trim; matching knife-pleated skirt with three bands of trim; cotton sleeveless blouse with V-shaped middy front. Original size 11 tag inside collar.

**333. BLUE WOOL TWILL MARINER COSTUME
WITH RED SATEEN COLLAR**
6" shoulder width. 13 1/4" waist. 7 1/2" skirt length. Ensemble comprises hip-length
jacket of blue wool twill with double row of pearl buttons, 3/4 sleeves, red muslin lining,
red cotton sateen mariner collar and cuffs with middy braid trim; and box-pleated short
skirt with attached sleeveless blouse having red sateen V-shaped bodice. Original size 11
tag inside collar.

334. WHITE LEATHER SHOES
3 3/4" L. Soft white lid leather shoes with stitched decoration have three sets of lacing
grommets, tan undersoles, partial original paper label.

335. BLACK OILED CLOTH MARINER'S HAT WITH "AU LOUVRE" LABEL
7" circular outside dimensions. 4" inside head width. Sailor-style cap of black oiled cloth
for waterproof protection has band decorated with black grosgrain ribbon and gold lettering "Lutin" (ship name).
Black silk twill lines the interior with gold stamp "Magasins du Louvre/Chapeaux".

336. NAVY BLUE LINEN MARINER SUIT
3" shoulder width. 5" waist. 5" skirt length. Three-piece ensemble of dark blue linen comprises short middy jacket which fits at waist above the skirt, large rounded collar, set-in sleeves, hook and eye closure at front; skirt with box pleats; and cap with muslin lining and red pompom. Each piece is generously trimmed with narrow ivory twill ribbon stripes.

337. NAVY BLUE WOOL FELT MARINER MIDDY, SKIRT AND CAP
4" shoulder width. 9" waist. 5 1/2" skirt length. Of heavy blue wool felt the ensemble comprises middy blouse with unusual full box-pleated sleeves, white wool cuffs, V-shaped collar which hooks closed in center, ivory silk twill bands; skirt with full gathers, double row of silk twill bands; cap with silk twill band and decoration, feather, cotton sateen lining.

338. CORDED BLUE WOOL MARINER COSTUME
6" shoulder width. 18" waist. 6" skirt length. Two-piece ensemble comprises blue corded wool pull-over middy blouse with laced front closure, 3/4 sleeves with sateen cuffs, large sateen collar with middy braid trim, brass anchor pin; and knife-pleated skirt with sleeveless sateen bodice.

339. PAIR, WOOL FLANNEL FROCKS AND MIDDY JACKETS
Each 6 1/4" shoulder width. 16" waist. 8 1/2" skirt length. Each matching ensemble comprises cream-colored wool flannel sleeveless frock with horizontal red pinstripes on bodice, vertical red pinstripes on drop-waist pleated skirt, muslin-lined bodice; and maroon wool flannel jacket with cotton pique shawl collar and wide cuffs, set-in full sleeves, one with large pearl buttons.

340. TWO WOOL SAILOR CAPS
3" and 4" inside head dimensions. Each of dark navy wool flannel with grosgrain ribbon bands; the larger with red pompom and rose cotton sateen lining; the smaller with muslin lining.

Mariner Costumes, 1890-1910

341. PAIR, WHITE WOOL KNIT SWEATER-COATS AND PLEATED SKIRTS
7" shoulder width. 15" waist. 8" skirt length. Pair of matching costumes, each comprising thick wool knit hip-length sweater with 3" turn-down collar, roll-up cuffs, double breasted effect with two rows of brass buttons, hip-belt at back with brass buttons; and pleated navy wool skirt, the manufacturer's basting stitches still intact. Size 11 tags sewn onto sweater backs. The ensembles were shown in Parisian department store catalogs of the 1910 era; the sizing referred to the SFBJ Bebe Jumeau.

342. WHITE CASHMERE MARINER COSTUME
3 1/4" shoulder width. 8" waist. 5 1/4" skirt length. Of cream-colored cashmere, the two-piece ensemble comprises double-breasted jacket with gathered waist, full gathered sleeves with blue catch-stitch embroidery at cuffs, blue silk satin middy-style collar; and knife-pleated skirt with blue silk satin border.

343. EIGHT-PIECE COTTON ENSEMBLE
7 1/2" shoulder width. 18" waist. 12" skirt length. Elaborately layered ensemble comprises white batiste frock with insert and border lace, elaborate construction including insert side-gathered panels, back-bodice tucks, blue silk satin sash; and cotton full slip with lace edging; cotton petticoat with 3" lace dust ruffle; white wool petticoat; cotton pantaloons, muslin chemise, blue silk stockings, blue leather shoes with silver buckles.

344. WHITE PIQUE PARTY DRESS WITH BONNET, SHOES AND STOCKINGS
7" shoulder width. 19" waist. 11" skirt length. Four-piece ensemble comprises white pique frock with elaborate Bertha collar above pleated bodice, very full sleeves, set-in waist, stitched-down back-bodice tucks, very elaborate overall trim of scalloped cutwork edging and inserts, rose silk ribbons interwoven into cutwork; and white batiste embroidered summer bonnet with 3" wired ruffled self-brim; and 5 1/2" L. rose leather shoes with six-pearl buttons and tacked-on leather soles; and 7" L. rose silk stockings with tatting and silk ribbon trim.

345. ROSE COTTON SATEEN SHOES
3" L. Pale rose cotton sateen shoes with rose overcast edging, delicate rose laces, silver buckles, tan undersoles.

346. ROSE COTTON SATEEN SHOES
3 1/4" L. Rose cotton sateen shoes with narrow twill banding, brass lacing grommets, rose laces, white leather undersoles signed 5.

347. MAGENTA SILK SHOES SIGNED H.H.
2 1/4" L. Magenta silk shoes with overcast edging, rose silk double buttons with loops, rose plush pompoms, dark tan undersoles signed H.H. (in heart) and 0, for Heinrich Handwerck.

348. ROSE AND CREAM MUSLIN TWO-PIECE SUIT
3" shoulder width. 9" length. Ensemble comprises rose and cream striped muslin blouson double-breasted jacket with 3/4 sleeves, banded neckline, and knife-pleated rose muslin skirt with button trim.

349. THREE-PIECE ENSEMBLE FOR TINY DOLL
2 1/4" shoulder width. 5" overall length. Set comprises white cotton frock with large bib yoke and double row of lace, gathered skirt with exposed pleated dust ruffle, hook and eye closure. With matching chemise and panties.

350. ROYAL GREEN VELVET BONNET
9" x 7 1/2" outside head dimensions. 3 1/2" inside head width. Buckram-shaped bonnet is covered with rich royal green velvet with wide wired brim, decorated with 2" W. rose silk moire rosettes and richly arranged bows, pleated rose silk moire on inside brim, ivory silk lining.

351. ROSE SILK BONNET
7 1/2" x 7 1/2" outside head dimensions. 3" inside head width. Buckram-shaped bonnet is covered with very delicate rose silk with pale stripes, has wired brim with additional gathered brim trimmed with embroidered lace; the inside brim decorated with two large rose silk rosettes and silver buckles.

352. TWO FAUX WATCHES AND PINS
3/4" watches. Gold-metal frames faux pocket watches have fancy faces, one back of embossed gilded metal, the other of blue enamel with floral design. Each watch with original watch pin designed to allow watch to be worn as decorative brooch.

353. DOLL ACCESSORIES
Comprising 1" W. gild metal circular purse with richly embossed design, chain handle, hinges open; rose enamel faux watch; tiny white enamel faux watch with floral designs and brass gilt brooch with blue enamel inlay and "Bebe".

Cotton Doll Dresses, Shoes, Bonnets And Accessories, 1890-1925

Cotton Doll Dresses, Shoes, Bonnets And Accessories, 1890-1925

353A. RED AND WHITE POLKA DOTTED PINAFORE
4" shoulder width. 12" waist. 10 1/2" overall length. Red cotton pinafore with white polka dots has Bertha collar, cotton braid trim on short sleeves, collar, yoke and hem, pleated front with attached pleated sash, open back except two buttons at top.

354. RED CHECKERED DRESS WITH DROP WAIST
6" shoulder width. 15 1/2" overall length. Red and white cotton dress with tiny checkered pattern has square-cut neck, dropped waist, set-in sleeves with cording at shoulder seams, gathered skirt, two pockets, red cotton trim at neck, waist, cuffs, faux-suspenders, hem, white feather-stitch embroidery, handkerchief, button back.

355: RED MUSLIN DRESS WITH SWISS EMBROIDERED TRIM
3 1/2" shoulder width. 10" overall length. Red cotton muslin chemise-style frock has fitted yoke, box-pleated front, set-in sleeves with ruched detail at shoulder seams, ruffled collar, Schiffli embroidery at collar, yoke, cuffs, and double row of hem ruffles, button back.

356. WHITE PIQUE PINAFORE
4 1/2" shoulder width. 11" overall length. White pique pinafore has square-cut neckline, bretelles with lace trim, full set-in sleeves with banded and lace-trimmed cuffs, pleated front with center box-pleat, two pockets with lace trim, belt, open back.

357. RED AND WHITE STRIPED FROCK
6" shoulder width. 17" overall length. Cotton dress of woven pattern of red and white stripes is intricately constructed in a manner to form solid blocks of red or white around the neckline and at the waist, with full gathers falling below, 3/4 sleeves with same stitched-down blocks and red banded cuffs.

358. TINY PLAID FROCK WITH EMBROIDERED COLLAR
2" width. 4" L. Red and white plaid cotton gingham frock has full box pleats hidden below 1" white cartridge-pleated collar with red scalloped overcast collar with cross-stitch detail, short puffed sleeves, white cord trim, hook and eye closure.

359. TINY EMBROIDERED ENSEMBLE
2" shoulder width. 3" L. Fine batiste cotton frock with dropped waist, demi-sleeves of lace, embroidered lace collar, 1/2" cross-stitched set-in waistband, double row of skirt ruffles with scalloped edges overcast in red and embroidered in blue and red, completely lined in muslin, tiny pearl buttons; and matching muslin chemise, panties and draw-string petticoat with delicate lace edging.

Cotton Doll Dresses, Shoes, Bonnets And Accessories, 1890-1925   109

360. RED WOOL FELT CAPE, WOVEN BONNET, AND JUMEAU SOCKS
About 6" shoulder width. Comprising red wool felt cape with five overcast rows of stitching, slightly flared border, rolled collar, silk lining. And red straw bonnet with elaborately turned-up brim edged in red silk, with red silk bows and fabric flowers; and red cotton knit socks for Bebe Jumeau.

361. RED WORSTED WOOL COAT
6" shoulder width. 14" overall length. Of fine bright red worsted wool with extended lapels and sailor collar edged in white stitching and gold braid, Juliet sleeves with box pleats at shoulders and cuffs, eight decorative gold buttons, hook and eye closure, cotton chintz lining.

362. BLACK LEATHER BEBE JUMEAU SHOES, SIZE 6
2 1/4". Black leather with brown stitching, gold bead button closure, brown silk ribbon trim, brown leather soles, marked with bee symbol, 6, and Paris Depose.

363. BLACK LEATHER BEBE JUMEAU SHOES, SIZE 7
2 1/2". Identical to #362 except slightly larger, marked 7, bee symbol and Paris Depose.
364. BLACK LEATHER SHOES SIGNED "BEBE JUMEAU DEPOSE 7"
2 1/2". Black leather with pronounced brown overcast stitching, silver button closure, brown silk rosette trim, brown undersoles, signed "Bebe Jumeau Depose 7".

365. BLACK LEATHER SHOES SIGNED "BEBE JUMEAU DEPOSE 9"
3 1/4". Black iridescent leather with pronounced brown overcast stitching, silver button closure, brown silk ribbons, tan undersoles, signed "Bebe Jumeau Depose 9".

366. BLACK LEATHER SHOES SIGNED "BEBE JUMEAU DEPOSE 11"
3 1/2". Identical to #364 except larger.

367. BLACK LEATHER SHOES FOR "RABERY"
4 1/4". Black leather shoes with silver button and loop closures have brown silk ribbon trim, leather soles, signed "Rabery Paris".

368. BLACK LEATHER SHOES SIGNED "BEBE JUMEAU DEPOSE 13"
4" L. Black leather with brown overcast edging, brown silk ankle ties, brown silk ribbon trim, brown soles signed "Bebe Jumeau Depose 13".

369. TWO WHITE PIQUE JACKETS
5 1/2" shoulder width. 8" length. Vertically ribbed white pique jackets have set-in long sleeves with braid at hems and cuffs, sailor collars with various Swiss embroidery or cutwork trim.

370. WHITE SWISS WOVEN PATTERNED COTTON FROCK AND PINAFORE
5" shoulder width. 16 3/4" waist. 8 3/4" skirt length. White swiss cotton frock with richly interwoven pattern has Bertha collar with scalloped edge trimmed in red overcast stitch, feather-stitched embroidery at yoke, collar and cuffs, gathered bodice with set-in waistband, full skirt, 3" self dust ruffle with red scalloped hemline. With matching pinafore.

371. WOVEN STRAW BONNET
7" circular outer dimensions. 2 1/4" inside head width.
Woven straw bonnet with very wide brim and flat top has silk ribbon binding and band, elaborate silk ribbon trim, muslin lining.

372. WOVEN STRAW BONNET
7" circular outer dimensions. 3" inside head width. Woven straw bonnet has wide brim, flat top, simple yet elegant decoration with ivory grosgrain silk banding, brim, streamers and buttons. Muslin lining, marked "7", produced for Bebe Jumeau.

Cotton Doll Dresses, Shoes, Bonnets And Accessories, 1890-1925 111

373. CREAM POLISHED COTTON FROCK WITH BLACK VELVET LACING

5 1/2" shoulder width. 12" waist. 12" skirt length. Of polished cotton the high-waist frock has set-in sleeves trimmed with black velvet and lace at cuffs, gathered skirt with double row of tatting and narrow black velvet cord at skirt, elaborate criss-cross of black velvet ribbons on front bodice, black velvet buttons.

374. CREAM COTTON PINAFORE DRESS WITH WHITE BLOUSE

7" shoulder width. 16" waist. 10" length. White cotton organza blouse with long-sleeves and front pleating is beneath a pale yellow (cream) pinafore dress printed with black wildflowers, with six rows of front tucking, black catch-stitch on neckline and sleeve edges, self-piped edges.

375. LACE BONNET

9" x 8" outside head dimensions. 5" inside head width. Bands of re-embroidered lace are constructed in a manner to form circular-shaped bonnet, cording detail, double ruffled mechlin lace brim with cutwork edging, wide ivory silk bows, silk lined.

376. WHITE DOTTED SWISS BONNET

8" circular outside dimensions. 3 1/2" inside head width. Designed to perch atop the head, the dotted swiss bonnet has handkerchief top with ruffled lace edging and medallion center, gathered sides, wire-strengthened brim of graduated width, lace ruffled edging, ivory silk band and bows.

377. LEMON EMBROIDERED COTTON LADY'S GOWN

6" shoulder width. 13" skirt length. Yellow cotton percale with white embroidered stripes, full-cut bodice with narrow pleats overlaid by wide Irish crochet collar, georgette trimmed plastron with horizontal rows of lace and black velvet, pouf short sleeves with lace and black velvet trim, bias-cut flared skirt with box pleats and slightly extended length in rear, black velvet sash and gold buckle.

378. IVORY SILK TWILL BONNET

6" x 6" outside head dimensions. 3" inside head width. Grosgrain-shaped bonnet is covered with ivory silk twill in pleats and gathers, has inlaid silk brocade ribbon, chiffon gathered brim, ivory silk ribbons and streamers, cotton sateen lining.

379. IVORY SILK BONNET

4" x 4" outside head dimensions. 1 1/2" inside head size. Wire-shaped bonnet with buckram form is covered with richly gathered ivory silk satin, wide brim with white georgette trimming the inside edge, ivory satin and flower decoration.

380. IVORY SILK BONNET WITH PLEATED RUFFLE

7" x 7" outside head dimension. 2" inside head size. Wire-shaped bonnet with buckram form is covered with box-pleated ivory silk satin, has double row of lace ruffles framing the face, 2 1/2" border of pleated muslin with lace edging, ivory silk ribbon loops.

Cotton Doll Dresses, Shoes, Bonnets And Accessories, 1890-1925

381. WHITE BATISTE BLOUSE

8" shoulder width. Delicate white batiste blouse has front and back yokes of guipure beading interwoven with ivory silk ribbons,
shirred lower bodice with lace fagoting, waist of guipure beading with silk grosgrain ribbon, balloon sleeves, double row of cutwork collar, lingerie buttons.

382. WHITE TULLE FROCK WITH IRISH CROCHET COLLAR AND TULLE CAP

7" shoulder width. 20" overall length. Sheer white tulle frock with full gathers below high waist, full sleeves decorated with soutache and tatting, 6 1/2" Bertha collar of Irish crochet with elaborate pattern of butterflies, bees and flowers, soutache braid on trim. With ivory tulle bonnet with inset lace banding and pleated lace-trimmed edging, peach silk ribbons.

383. WHITE NAINSOOK COTTON FROCK AND CHARLOTTE BONNET

5 1/2" shoulder width. 13" overall length. Summer dress constructed of alternate 1" bands of nainsook cotton and insertion lace, fitted waist, stand-up collar, bishop sleeves, wide bretelles of lace and embroidered banding, fagoting at waist, pin-tucks at back, button closure; and dotted Swiss muslin Charlotte or mobcap with ruffled and lace-edged brim, silk ribbon band.

384. CREAM VOILE FROCK WITH YELLOW ROSES PRINT

4 1/2" shoulder width. 10 1/2" waist. 10 1/2" skirt length. Cream-colored voile with woven stripes and delicate yellow roses and lavender ribbons printed onto fabric, tulle bodice with re-embroidered flowers, lace collar and cuffs, narrow silk ribbons, cartridge pleated full skirt.

385. PALE YELLOW VOILE FROCK WITH DELICATE FLORAL PRINT

4" shoulder width. 8" waist. 8" skirt length. Of very delicate cotton voile, the frock is printed with delicate blue and peach colored wildflowers, has pleated yoke, gathered collar, bretelles, full sleeves with 1" cuffs, full bodice, gathered waist, hook and eye closure.

386. THREE PAIRS OF COTTON SOCKS

2 1/2" foot size. 4" H. Woven cotton socks with woven-in heels and toes have woven design at knees.

387. BLUE ETAMINE COTTON FROCK IN KATE GREENAWAY STYLE
5" shoulder width. 13" overall length. Delicate cotton with woven drawnwork and blue band has high waist, deep V-shaped bodice with bretelle collar, bishop sleeves, pleated skirt, Bavarian lace bodice, and 1" lace edging on collar and cuffs, Austrian glass buttons, hook and eye closure.

388. WHITE MULL OVERDRESS ON BLUE MUSLIN LINER
3 1/2" shoulder width. 10" overall length. Sheer mull overdress over blue muslin liner, with blouson dropped waist, square-cut neckline, double tiered skirt, elbow-length puffed sleeves, torchon lace trim, hook and eye closure.

389. WHITE COTTON 'DRAP D'ETE' SUMMER FROCK
9" shoulder width. 12" overall length. Delicate white cotton summer frock with woven illusion dots has rounded neck and short sleeves banded in 1" blue cotton sateen, drop waist, bodice panel of guipure lace with Valenciennes lace inset, gathered waist, hook and eye closure.

390. BLACK LEATHER SHOES WITH BROWN ROSETTES
4". Iridescent black kid leather shoes with white stitching have double black-bead ankle buttons, silver buckle trim, brown silk floss rosettes, stamped "4".

391. BLACK LEATHER SHOES BY ALART, SIZE 6
2 1/3" L. Black leather shoes with pierced hole design have black silk ribbon ties, tan undersoles with symbol of doll in chemise, registered by Alart in Paris in 1913.

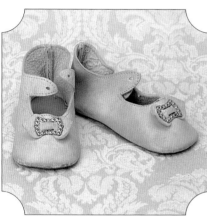

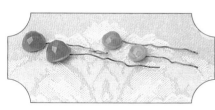

392. WOVEN STRAW BONNET
3 1/2" x 4". Blue and natural woven straw bonnet with turned-up brim at back is decorated with blue plaid silk ribbon band and bows, tiny fabric flowers, muslin lining.

393. BLUE SOFT KID LEATHER SHOES
4" L. Pale blue soft kid leather shoes have straps for bow ties, leather trim with silver buckles, tan undersoles.

394. TWO PAIR OF BEBE JUMEAU EARRINGS
In turquoise and rose glass beads with copper wire for insertion into pierced ear holes.

395. WIRED VOILE PALE AQUA SUNBONNET
7" x 6" outside head dimensions. 2 1/2" inside head dimensions.
Aqua delicate patterned voile cotton with shadowed interwoven details has cup-shaped back with pleated bavolet, 4" brim comprising 1" gathered bands with cording between, valenciennes lace edging, long self-fabric ties with lace-edging all around and feather-stitch trim.

396. PALE BLUE COTTON CHEMISE FROCK
5 1/2" shoulder width. 12" overall length. Pale blue homespun cotton chemise-style frock has fitted yoke above full-length box-pleated front and back held by lace trimmed sash, white feather stitching on the banded collar, cuffs, pocket, yoke, hem, and belt; lace edging on collar, belt, and cuffs, tiny hand-kerchief in breast pocket.

397. BLUE COTTON CHAMBRAY TWO-PIECE SUIT
5 1/2" shoulder width. 13" waist. 6 1/4" skirt. Of navy blue cotton chambray, the suit comprises knife-pleated skirt with four rows of middy braid and fleurette embroidery, scalloped overcast hemline; and long semi-fitted jacket with V-shaped middy collar and cuffs, each trimmed with four rows of middy braid and embroidered fleurettes.

398. INDIGO SWISS MUSLIN PINAFORE
4 1/2" shoulder width. 14" waist. 11 1/2" overall length.   Indigo blue Swiss muslin pinafore with open back, pleated front, low rounded collar, stitched-on sash, demi-sleeves, pockets and hem of darker blue Swiss embroidery with white edelweiss flowers, white contrast stitching overall.

399. NAVY BLUE COTTON FROCK
4 1/2" shoulder width. 12" waist. 5" skirt length. Navy blue cotton frock has fitted bodice with tucks at front, box-pleats at back, Schiffli white embroidered panels at front which match the rounded scalloped collar, cuffs, hemline and pocket trim, set-in sleeves, full gathered skirt, two pockets, back waist ties.

400. TWO-PIECE ENSEMBLE WITH PRINTED "CHILDREN AND DOLLS" MUSLIN BLOUSE

6" shoulder width. 12" waist. 10 3/4" skirt length. Comprising muslin blouse with long balloon sleeves, cartridge pleating at shoulders, front and back box-pleats, one front pleated panel disguising the hook and eye closure, stand-up collar; the blouse printed in unique design of children playing with dolls and puppy. With grey cotton sateen skirt having feather stitching on hem and rosette trim.

401. BLUE CHAMBRAY CHEMISE-STYLED PINAFORE
6 1/4" shoulder width. 16 3/4" overall length. Blue cotton chambray pinafore in chemise style has low neckline with rounded diamond-point collar trimmed with double row of embroidered banding and zig-zag, set-in sleeves with same trim, two pockets with embroidered bands, bands and zig-zag at hemline and along the back seams, the back buttoned to waist and open below.

402. EMBROIDERED COTTON BLUE AND WHITE FROCK
5 1/2" shoulder width. 18" waist. 10" skirt length. White cotton with interwoven counterpane pattern in blue and white has embroidered blue dots, rounded collar with lace trim, re-embroidered cutwork yoke, full bodice, fitted piped waist, bishop sleeves with set-in cuffs, gathered skirt, button and loop closure.

403. WHITE COTTON FROCK WITH BLUE EMBROIDERED CUTWORK
7" waist. 19" overall length. White cotton summer frock with rounded neckline, corded dropped waist with loose fit, pleated and shirred bodice inset flanked by 1 1/2" bands of re-embroidered broderie Anglaise in royal blue; demi-sleeves and 2" collar with matching cutwork trim, gathered skirt with 6" band of blue embroidered cutwork and scalloped edging, pin tucks and button closure at back, hand-embroidered detail on front bodice.

404. WOVEN STRIPED COTTON SUNDRESS
6" shoulder width. 16" waist. 13" overall length. White on white-striped cotton sleeveless sundress has rounded neckline, criss-cross yoke, press-pleated lower bodice, drop waist, gathered lower skirt, box-pleated back bodice, blue Swiss embroidery at neckline, yoke, sleeves and hemline, buttoned back.

405. PRINTED COTTON PARASOL WITH WOODEN HANDLE
16" L. Wooden-handled parasol with bone handle, silver tip and bands, metal frame which works, has original printed muslin cotton cover depicting garlands of fruit, 2" woven swiss embroidered cotton border.

406. WHITE PATTERNED LAWN SUNBONNET
8" x 6" outside head dimensions. 3 1/2" inside head dimensions. Delicate lawn bonnet with narrowest interwoven stripes and blue dots has full gathered back, pleated brim extending from back of head, box-pleated bavolet, lace edging, self-fabric ties with lace edging and blue featherstitch embroidery.

407. AQUA KNIT CAPELET AND PLUSH VELVETEEN CAP
11" neckline, 6" length. Aqua baby yarn knit capelet with knotted edging and pompom trim around neck, front and edge. Twisted yarn ties with tassels. Navy plush velveteen cap measures 11 1/2" inside head dimensions. Wider front than back. Aqua satin ribbon and rosette trim. Printed cotton brocade lining.

408. AQUA GEORGETTE BONNET
5 1/2" x 3 1/2" outside head dimensions. 3" inside head dimensions. Buckram-stiffened bonnet has white batiste covering, the brim richly decorated with ruched and box-pleated aqua georgette, georgette ties.

409. AQUA WOOL KNIT JACKET AND BONNET
5" shoulder width. 9" L. Delicately-knit aqua wool jacket has set-in sleeves, scalloped neckline with drawstring, deeply scalloped hemline. And matching bonnet with scalloped neck, ribbon-candy woven trim, aqua silk ribbons and streamers.

410. WHITE FUR MUFF AND STOLE
4" muff. Luxurious white fur muff with black fox tails has rose silk padded lining, rose cord neck tie; with matching fox head and fox tail stole.

411. WOVEN COTTON FINGERLESS ELBOW GLOVES
10" L. Woven off-white cotton gloves with fancy pattern are elbow length, defined wrist, scalloped edging at fingers, defined thumbs.

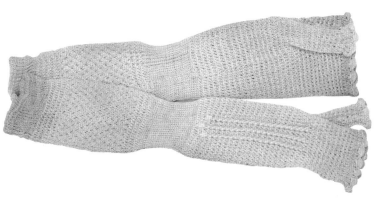

412. BROWN WOOL FLANNEL JACKET AND STRAW BONNET
4" shoulder width. 10" L. Light-brown wool double-breasted jacket has deep collar with guipure edging, set-in sleeves with guipure edging, double-breasted effect with one row of white pearl buttons, ivory silk twill lining. And straw bonnet with upturned brim, ivory silk band, bow and edging.

413. TAUPE WOOL FLANNEL COAT AND LEGGINGS
6" shoulder width. 12 1/2" overall length. Taupe wool flannel double-breasted coat has wide lapels, rolled collar, set-in sleeves with shoulder pleats, double row of brass buttons, rose silk twill lining. And wool knit leggings with defined ankles, foot straps, top-of-foot covers, pearl buttons.

414. TAN LEATHER BOOTS BY ALART, SIZE 6
2 1/2" L. Light-tan leather high boots with cream-colored overcast edges, three pairs each of lacing grommets, original laces, tan leather soles with maker's mark of doll in chemise, for Alart of Paris.

415. BLACK LEATHER SADDLE SHOES
3". Black leather saddle shoes have scalloped edges, three pairs of lacing grommets, black laces, (replaced) soles.

416. LIGHT-TAN SADDLE SHOES
2 1/2". Light-tan soft kid leather shoes have pierced hole design, scalloped edge, triple pair of brass-edged lacing grommets, original laces, signed "4".

417. BLACK LEATHER SADDLE SHOES
2". Black leather saddle shoes have soft tan leather inserts, brown stitching, double pair of lacing grommets, brown laces, tan undersoles.

418. BROWN SADDLE SHOES
1 3/4" L. Brown shoes with saddle-style shape have pierced hole design, double lacing grommets, original brown lacing, white undersoles signed "1".

419. BLACK SCHOENHUT SHOES
2" L. Black soft kid leather shoes have white stitching, silver buckles, twill laces, two grommeted holes in soles of each.

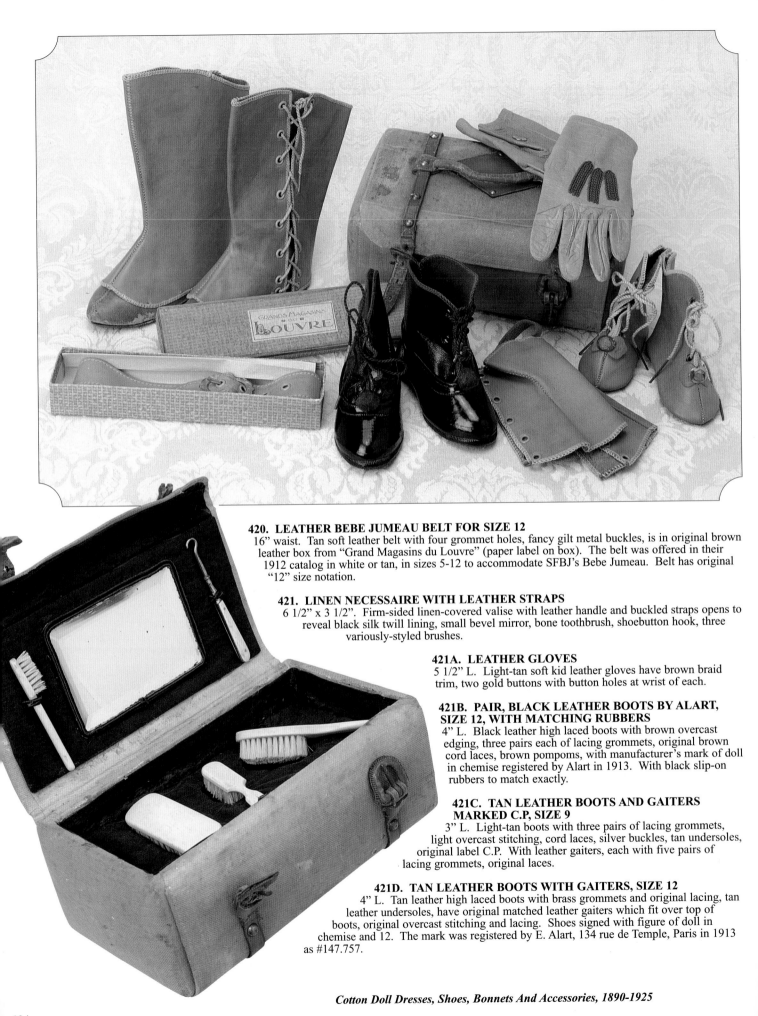

420. LEATHER BEBE JUMEAU BELT FOR SIZE 12

16" waist. Tan soft leather belt with four grommet holes, fancy gilt metal buckles, is in original brown leather box from "Grand Magasins du Louvre" (paper label on box). The belt was offered in their 1912 catalog in white or tan, in sizes 5-12 to accommodate SFBJ's Bebe Jumeau. Belt has original "12" size notation.

421. LINEN NECESSAIRE WITH LEATHER STRAPS

6 1/2" x 3 1/2". Firm-sided linen-covered valise with leather handle and buckled straps opens to reveal black silk twill lining, small bevel mirror, bone toothbrush, shoebutton hook, three variously-styled brushes.

421A. LEATHER GLOVES

5 1/2" L. Light-tan soft kid leather gloves have brown braid trim, two gold buttons with button holes at wrist of each.

421B. PAIR, BLACK LEATHER BOOTS BY ALART, SIZE 12, WITH MATCHING RUBBERS

4" L. Black leather high laced boots with brown overcast edging, three pairs each of lacing grommets, original brown cord laces, brown pompoms, with manufacturer's mark of doll in chemise registered by Alart in 1913. With black slip-on rubbers to match exactly.

421C. TAN LEATHER BOOTS AND GAITERS MARKED C.P, SIZE 9

3" L. Light-tan boots with three pairs of lacing grommets, light overcast stitching, cord laces, silver buckles, tan undersoles, original label C.P. With leather gaiters, each with five pairs of lacing grommets, original laces.

421D. TAN LEATHER BOOTS WITH GAITERS, SIZE 12

4" L. Tan leather high laced boots with brass grommets and original lacing, tan leather undersoles, have original matched leather gaiters which fit over top of boots, original overcast stitching and lacing. Shoes signed with figure of doll in chemise and 12. The mark was registered by E. Alart, 134 rue de Temple, Paris in 1913 as #147.757.

Cotton Doll Dresses, Shoes, Bonnets And Accessories, 1890-1925

422. US MAIL BAG AND WWI RATIONS BAG
3 1/2" x 2". US Mail bag is of heavy canvas with tan leather flap closure, stamped "US Mail". And 2 1/2" x 1 1/2" French muslin rations bag with leather strap containing assortment of foodstuffs for soldier, viz. sardines, canned meats, jerky, box of matches, towels, stationery, green knit socks and pipe. Marked "Depose" on bag.

423. WOVEN COTTON DOLL SOCKS
In various sizes, 3 1/2" - 4 1/2" H. Loosely-woven patterns in colors of brown, mauve, magenta, cream and tan.

424. WHITE FUR STOLE IN ORIGINAL AU BON MARCHE BOX
13" overall length. 7" L. box. White fur fox stole with amber glass eyes, black fox tail, is enclosed in original box with Au Bon Marche label for "fourrures" (furs).

425. BLACK VELVET BERET WITH MAGENTA SILK RIBBONS
6 1/2" circular outer dimensions. 4" inside head width. Black velvet beret with wire-stiffened band, magenta silk bow, silk lining. And 7" width padded fur muff with silk lining, cord.

425A. WHITE LEATHER FRENCH SHOES WITH MAKER'S MARK
2 3/4" l. Soft white kid leather shoes have three pairs of lacing grommets, pierced design around upper edge, original laces, leather soles marked with symbol of boot and "8 Modele depose", one shoe with original paper label "Made in France".

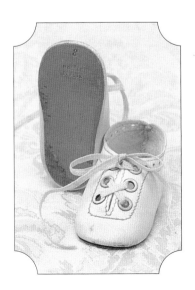

Cotton Doll Dresses, Shoes, Bonnets And Accessories, 1890-1925

426. LACE CHARLOTTE BONNET
9" circular outer dimensions. 3 1/2" inside head width. Aqua silk mob cap has tatting cover, double lace brim of broderie Anglaise and fine edged re-embroidered tulle, aqua georgette brim, bow and streamers with ruched edging.

427. TULLE AND LACE CHARLOTTE BONNET
9" circular outer dimensions. 2 1/2" inside head dimensions. Wire-framed bonnet in mobcap style has very wide brim with bands of tulle and shadow lace, padded cap top over buckram form, muslin lining, aqua silk ribbon trim.

428. COTTON WINDOW-PANE PLAID FROCK
6" shoulder width. 14" overall length. White cotton frock with black window-pane printed design has squared bias-cut neckline, dropped waist with stitched-on bias-cut belt at sides and back, knife-pleated skirt, kimono sleeves with pleating at the bias-cut cuffs, grey fabric edging, pearl button closure and decoration.

429. PALE GREY "DRAP D'ETE" SUMMER FROCK
5" shoulder width. 11" overall length. Delicate pale grey frock with interwoven flecks has square-cut low neckline, kimono sleeves with sewn-

430. VOILE SUMMER FROCK WITH PASTEL PRINT
5 1/2" shoulder width. 13" overall length. Sheer voile frock with delicate floral print
in pastels has surplice front panel with hook and eye closure, dropped waist, pleated
short skirt, 3/4 kimono sleeves; the flap, waistband and sleeve edges trimmed with 1
1/2" galloon lace in airy open fashion and edged with lavender silk ribbons, matching
bow at belt closure.

431. VOILE SUMMER FROCK WITH VIOLET PRINT
5 1/2" shoulder width. 13" overall length. Printed voile frock with delicate printed
design of violets and leaves has loose-fitting chemise style, kimono sleeves, full-length
front and back pleats, Buster Brown style collar, cuffs and tie in lavender polished
cotton, hidden buttons under front pleat.

432. CLOCHE WIRE-FRAMED NET BONNET
9" x 7" outside dimensions. 3" inside head width. Wire-framed cloche-style bonnet
has tiered layers of pleated loosely-woven net covering the entire bonnet and forming a
ruffle around the bottom edge, trimmed with lavender silk band and fabric miniature
lilac flowers.

Cotton Doll Dresses, Shoes, Bonnets And Accessories, 1890-1925

433. ROSE COMBED MUSLIN PINAFORE AND SUNBONNET
5 1/2" shoulder width. 13" overall length. Soft rose pinafore of fine quality muslin has rounded neckline with feather stitch detail, 1 1/2" collar with insertion lace trimmed with rose silk ribbon and scalloped lace edging, demi-sleeves and lace edging with same ribbon and lace edging, open back; and straw sunbonnet with rose cotton sateen backing, bavolet, ruffled brim.

434. COTTON ORGANDY FROCK WITH ROSE PATTERN
6" shoulder width. 16" overall length. Sheer cream organdy summer frock with delicately printed roses, fitted yoke above gathers, undefined waist, set-in gathered short sleeves, organdy rounded collar and turned up sleeve bands trimmed with delicate lace, organdy front placket with rose feather-stitched edging pearl buttons and loops.

435. TWO DIMITY COTTON BONNETS
Each 2 1/2" inside head width. Of identical fabric with delicately printed tiny roses, one is Charlotte or mobcap with ruffled lace-edge brim and peach silk band and bow; other is sunbonnet with gathered bands, lace edging, long lace-edged self ties, feather-stitched trim.

436. WHITE CUTWORK CHARLOTTE BONNET
10" outside head dimensions. 3 1/2" inside head size. White Swiss cutwork mobcap-style bonnet is elaborately constructed with wide bands of cutwork, center panel of tiny tucks, 2" gathered cutwork brim with wire-strengthening over pleated dust ruffle with lace edging, rose silk banding with tiny fabric flowers, muslin lining.

437. ROSE SILK TAFFETA BONNET
12" circ. outside dimensions. 4 1/2" inside head width. Buckram-shaped bonnet with wire-shaped brim is covered with scalloped-edged rose silk taffeta (frail), unusual woven straw brim and medallion top, 2" net overlay with re-embroidered edging, muslin pleated lining.

438. PALE GREEN COTTON PINAFORE
6" shoulder width. 14" overall length. Delicate pale green cotton pinafore printed with design of young girl in sailor costume playing jump rope has fitted bodice hidden under 2" ruffled collar with Valenciennes lace trim, ruffled capelet-style sleeves with lace trim, open back with two upper pearl buttons.

439. CHINESE SILK COSTUME
3 1/2" shoulder width. 8" waist. 6" pants length. Comprising green silk kimono-style jacket with embroidered detail of boy playing with frog, cording at outside edges, frog closures with blue glass bead buttons, fully lined; and 3/4 length royal blue silk pants with gold thread embroidery and cording at hem.

440. IVORY AND AQUA SILK PIERROT COSTUME
11" shoulder width. 17" jacket length. 22" waist (adjustable). Ivory silk costume comprises long jacket with wide ruffled and fringed collar of patterned blue silk, ivory placket, pockets and long sleeves edged with blue fringed silk, blue silk-covered buttons, full muslin lining, hook and eye closure. With matching short pants and wire-framed net-lined cap. In original box from Au Louvre department store in Paris.

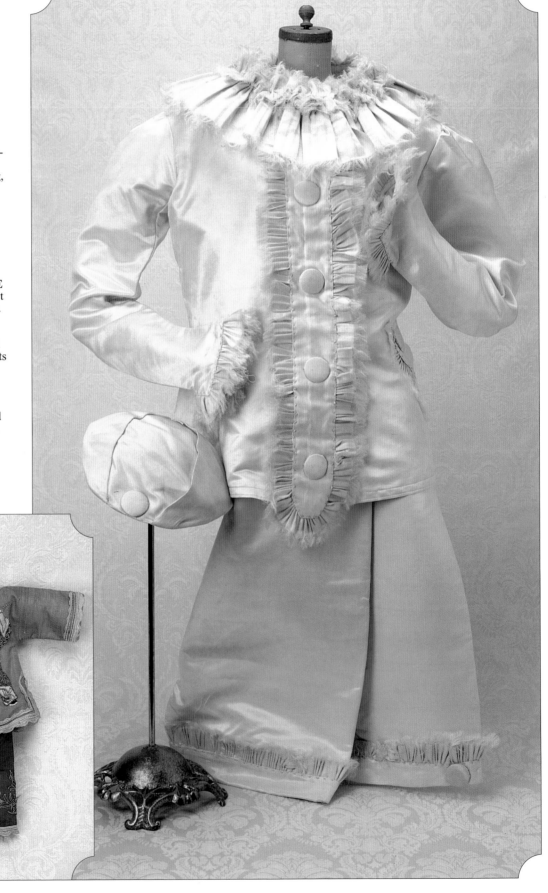

441. CHILD'S FRENCH SEWING NECESSAIRE
15" x 10". Blue paper-covered box opens to reveal luxury interior with red silk lining, multitude of compartments, and bottom drawer; containing many sewing and needlework tools, yarns, threads, bobbins, samplers, partially worked tapestries, glass beads. The box exterior is decorated with brass ormulu mounts and handle.

442. CHILD'S FRENCH SEWING ENSEMBLE "TAPISSERIE"
10" x 7". A hard-sided paper-covered box with purple iris design labelled "tapisserie" hinges open to reveal interior containing needlework frame, various samples of completed needlework, samples of embroidery trim, threads, yarns, design samples, and "bon points" (hand-dated 1899) with good behavior messages; pull-out bottom drawer.

443. CHILD'S FRENCH SEWING ENSEMBLE "MAGASIN DE PERLES"
14" x 10". A hard-sided paper covered box hinges open to reveal well-fitted interior with number of glass-topped boxes containing various color glass beads, tapestry, yarns, needlework samples, scissors, silver needle case and hook, and scales for weighing beads.

444. CHILD'S FRENCH SEWING ENSEMBLE
9" x 6". A hard-sided paper covered box labelled "mercerie" hinges open to reveal well-fitted interior with sewing tools, stencils, threads, scissors, embroidery yarns, snaps, buttons, needles, and half-finished actual alphabet sampler; has lift-out tray.

445. CHILD'S FRENCH ENSEMBLE "TABLEAUX DE PERLES"
13" x 8". A hard-sided paper-covered box labelled "tableaux de perles" contains numerous glass-topped little boxes, wooden embroidery hoop, tapestries, threads, and more.

446. PAPER FORTUNE-TELLING SKIRT
8 1/2" L. Designed to be worn under the fabric skirt of fortune telling doll, the folding paper leaves each contain a hand-script fortune, skirt comprising several hundred leaves.

447. GREY WOOL FLANNEL UNIFORM CAP
4 1/2" x 5" outside head dimensions. 3" inside head width. Grey wool flannel cap has periwinkle blue piping and band, black leather brim, brass emblem, muslin lining.

448. BLACK COTTON PLAY SUIT EMBROIDERED B.P.
6" shoulder width. Black cotton tunic with red edging and flared shape has monogram B.P. on front, with matching short pants.

449. BLACK VELVET TAM
2" head width. Of black velvet with red plaid trim, the tam is authentically styled and decorated.

450. BLACK COTTON SATEEN PINAFORE AND MUSLIN DRESS

4" shoulder width. 9" length. Maroon striped muslin sleeveless dress with reverse pattern on bodice and skirt has scalloped collar, black cotton sateen pinafore with set-in gathered sleeves, cuffs, box-pleated front and back. Included is black velvet sash with buckle.

451. BLACK WOOL UNIFORM CAP

3 1/2" x 4". 3" inside head dimensions. Unlined black wool cap has stiffened wide band with band lining, narrow black leather brim, brass buttons with neck strap, brass petal emblem, paper label "3" on interior.

452. GENTLEMAN'S FORMALWEAR ENSEMBLE

3 1/2" shoulder width. 8" waist. 8" pant length. Comprising white cotton long-sleeved shirt with front panel tucks and pearl buttons; vest with constructed collar, double-breasted pearl buttons; lined black wool flannel dinner jacket with long tails and full silk lining, lapels and buttons; and matching trousers with fly front, decorative stripe on side seams.

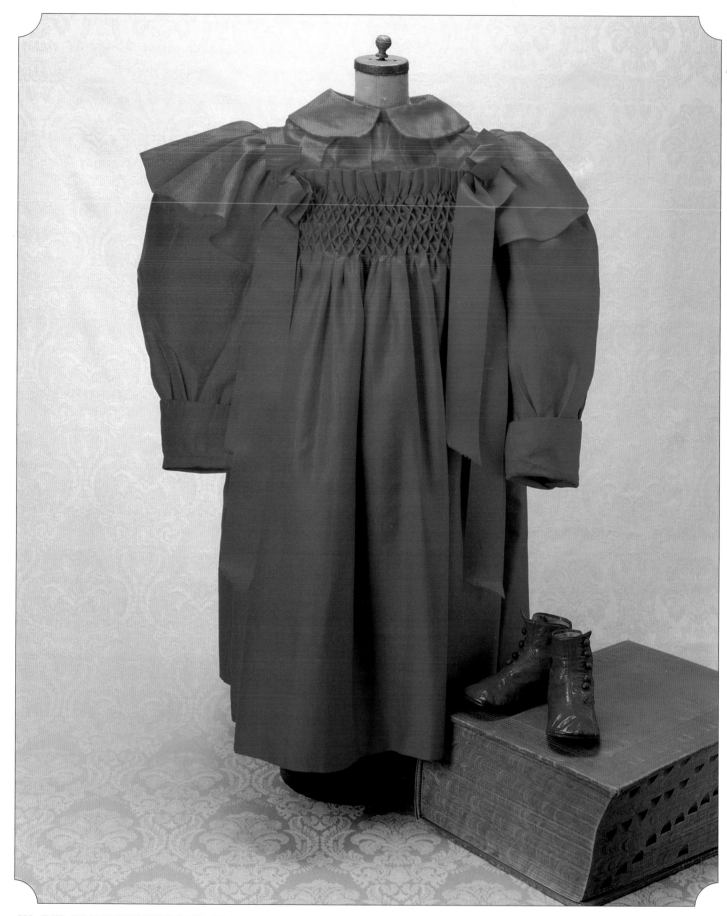

453. RED SILK PARTY DRESS AND LEATHER HIGH-BUTTON SHOES
9" collar. 26" full length. Rich red silk party frock has rounded collar, gathered yoke above richly smocked detail constructed to appear as though a separate pinafore, full skirt falls from smocking, very full set-in sleeves, long red silk ribbon streamers; the construction is repeated on the backside. The dress is fully lined in red cotton chintz. And 5" L. red leather five-button boots with tacked-in tan leather soles.

Index